VILLA

VOLVO

VOVVE

LYS
www.lysforlag.com
Editorial office: redaktion@lysforlag.com
Project manager: Sofi Tegsveden Deveaux
Cover and book design: Sofi Tegsveden Deveaux

ISBN 978-91-89141-31-5

Villa Volvo Vovve

ED. CATHERINE EDWARDS
& EMMA LÖFGREN

The Local's Word Guide
to Swedish Life

LYS

TO THE LOCAL'S READERS

This book is for you, if you've ever wanted to learn about Sweden beyond Abba and meatballs

---

Please connect and tell us what your favourite Swedish word is, how you fail to pronounce *fy*, and where to find the most delicious *dammsugare*.

thelocal.se @thelocalsweden
lysforlag.com @lysandelagom

#swedelife #swedishvvv

Foreword

Shigeyuki Hiroki, Ambassador of Japan to Sweden

Language is key to understanding people and culture. When I came to Sweden, I felt the urge to gain insight into different aspects of Swedish thinking by meeting Swedes in every corner of the country. Fortunately, I have been able to visit all 21 counties in Sweden, *från Ystad till Haparanda.*

It is sometimes misunderstood that diplomats would only meet with the VIPs of a country. However, it is imperative for us to communicate with a diverse variety of people in the posted country such as artists, musicians, teachers, scholars, students, fishermen, farmers, innovators, healthcare workers and so on. Each individual has a unique personal aura coming from his or her upbringing and the community or culture they belong to, so every person I have met so far has taught me something new and interesting about Sweden.

On top of that, luckily with the help of social media, I was able to acquaint myself with some interesting Swedish words, especially through reading The Local's 'Swedish word of the day', the online article series that inspired this book. Some of my personal favourites are *hunddagis*, *deckare* and *snapsvisa*. The *snapsvisa* is a tradition that I am particularly fond of, as it brings to me many memories of Swedish friends, coworkers and acquaintances, happily bursting into song together as we gather to celebrate one of the many Swedish holidays.

Another phrase that has stayed with me is *mellan hägg och syrén* ('between the bird cherry and the lilac'). This phrase entails the spirit of the season, captures the Swedish appreciation of nature and the feeling of joy and freedom connected to the Swedish school graduation ceremony, which traditionally takes place in this specific period. It also conveys the jubilating joy the Swedes feel to welcome the summer season after enduring a long winter.

Yet another example is the proverb *envar sin egen lyckas smed.* The meaning of this proverb ('every man is the blacksmith of his own fortune') really opened my eyes to one of the secret keys to understanding Swedish success stories. To me, it speaks of Swedish diligence, orderliness, punctuality, honesty, perseverance and reservedness. I am also impressed by the Swedish people's affection to nature, *allemansrätten*, and their love of queuing.

Having been taught these various words and phrases by the people I've met in my years in Sweden, some physically and some via Twitter and Instagram, I strongly feel that I have gained a deeper insight into the joys and beliefs of the Swedish people. In this way, I feel that language can sometimes help me decipher the mindset of the people.

I intend to keep exploring the sea of Swedish culture to enrich myself and to promote mutual understanding between Japan and Sweden.

Discover the Scandinavian secrets
Introduction by the editor

Until recently, not many Swedish words were known outside the country, with just a few of its words adopted elsewhere, most of them fairly unexciting: 'orienteering', 'ombudsman', 'smorgasbord'. For many people overseas, their only interaction with Swedish was laughing at the labels in an Ikea store. When I moved to Stockholm in 2015, I didn't know much more than *hej*.

But then a trend for Scandinavian culture swept the globe, boosted by surveys showing their populations to be the world's happiest, most equal, or boasting the best quality of life. Two words in particular were catapulted to linguistic stardom: *fika* and *lagom*, roughly 'coffee break' and 'just the right amount'. Magazine articles and books debate whether the words themselves give us an insight into some 'Swedish secret' of how to live.

But there is much more to Sweden than *fika* and *lagom*. The title of this book, *Villa Volvo Vovve,* literally means '(detached) house, Volvo car, dog' and is a Swedish phrase used to joke about the typical, *lagom* middle class goals of adulthood. Nothing flashy, just a small house — this phrase pre-dates urban Sweden's current crowded and expensive housing market — a no-nonsense car and a pet.

Exploring everything that makes Sweden what it is, has been

our goal at *The Local* since 2004. Today it's a news organisation covering Europe's news in English across several countries, but it all started as a weekly email in 2004, when the company's co-founder, Paul, started sending short explanations of Sweden's news to classmates from his language class.

Although the company has grown, it's still fuelled by a desire to help foreign residents navigate life in their new home town, through the news, but also guides to housing, careers, and language. We understand what it's like to feel as if you're the only one who doesn't know the unwritten rules.

In 2018, we started our *Word of the Day* series to introduce our readers to the Swedish words that help you crack these cultural codes. We delved into a mixture of topical words that were making headlines, specifically Scandinavian concepts, and those little filler words that just help you sound more Swedish.

International readers told us how the words have helped as icebreakers with colleagues or in-laws. Native speakers got in touch to say they enjoyed learning something new about a word they use regularly (and even gave corrections or alternative viewpoints!). People suggested words they wanted us to explain, or quibbled over the examples we chose. It was great! Language belongs to all of us.

The words we chose for this book, all initially part of the *Word of the Day* series, are aimed at exploring the Swedish mindset and lifestyle, and we've added additional material to help you get under the skin of the country and its language.

Sweden, like any country, is a mass of contradictions: long summer nights and dark cold winters; expansive forest but technologically advanced cities; a liberal democracy but with harsh drug and alcohol policies.

Words like *kanelbullens dag* ('Cinnamon Bun Day'), *badkruka* ('bathing coward'), and *tvättstugelapp* ('passive-aggressive note left in the communal laundry room') may not have caught on worldwide, but they each help you get closer to understanding not only Sweden, Swedish, and the Swedes but also what it is like being human, anywhere and everywhere.

One thing I've learned at *The Local* is that you can almost never translate the news word for word. It doesn't work. A word that means something concrete to Swedes — whether it's the name of a political party, national holiday, or a common custom — needs context.

So what about untranslatable words? If you think about it long enough — and as a word nerd, I absolutely have — you could argue that most words are untranslatable. *Fika* might have a slightly different definition from 'coffee break', but the exact meaning depends at least as much on who is talking as what language they are speaking.

Many concepts don't translate perfectly between people even if they're speaking the same language. I've not seen anyone argue that 'coffee' is untranslatable, yet go to a cafe in different countries and ask for a coffee, and you're almost guaranteed to be presented with three different drinks: black filter coffee in Sweden, an espresso in Italy, and so on.

If you describe someone as 'punctual', you might be using a different definition than a Swede, even if *punktlig* is in the dictionary as a direct translation. Someone from India or China might laugh at the small size of a settlement that is called a 'city' here in Sweden. The list goes on. We all make assumptions based on our personal context every day.

And then there are idioms, those parts of language that mean something different from the sum of their words. Phrases like 'to slide in on a banana peel' or 'like the cat around hot porridge' are direct translations of Swedish idioms, but even if you knew each of the individual words, you'd have a slim chance of understanding what they meant (see *halka* and *gröt* for an explanation).

As for *fika* and *lagom*, you won't find them in this book as there are other, excellent books out there that explore these words in detail. To me, these are the language equivalent of a showy restaurant that tourists love, but locals are bemused by its inclusion in guides. Exciting, but there's so much more to see as well.

So if you're the type of person who prefers to try to get lost when they visit new places, and seeks out the scruffier but charming bars and cafes, then this is the book for you.

You'll learn how to greet people, compliment or insult them, how to navigate some of Sweden's beloved traditions, and talk about the weather, and food. We will look at how to use the words, when to avoid them, and explore the history of how they came to be. You'll learn about Sweden beyond the headlines, beyond the tourist guides, the good, the bad, and the bizarre.

This book will help you if you're travelling to Sweden, or even living there, to understand what's going on around you. But it's also a handbook for anyone who wants to embrace the Nordic way of life. Who knows, maybe you'll even discover the elusive Scandinavian secrets to happiness along the way.

Catherine Edwards
September 2021

A note on pronunciation

This is not a textbook. There are no obligations, no homework, no need to perform. But we know that some of our readers are curious and want to learn more. One of these things is pronunciation; how do you actually *say* those words? Therefore we have created audio files that you can access on lysforlag.com/vvv. To give you an indication of the diversity of the Swedish language, we have provided three different dialects, from the south and the north of Sweden, as well as Stockholm.

Listen carefully. Your brain may trick you. We hear things that are not there, because we expect them, and we miss other sounds because they are unfamiliar to our ears. Swedes who speak English often pronounce 'ice' and 'eyes' the same, because the voiced *s* ('eyes') doesn't exist in Swedish. Our brains filter it out and replace it with the closest equivalent, the unvoiced *s* ('ice'). Likewise, your ears may not be tuned into the nuances of Swedish sounds, and you may unconsciously add a voiced *s* where it shouldn't be, for example between vowels in *musik*, or in conjunction with other voiced consonants such as *g* in *lördagsgodis* or *v* in *Sverige*.

If you are new to Swedish, you may be stunned by the *tj* in *tjej*, *tjena* and *tjomme*, thinking this is where the real challenge is. In fact, this sound — often spelled *tj* or *k* (ɕ in the International Phonetic Alphabet [IPA]) — is not that different from the *sh* in the English 'sheep'. Likewise the *sj* — ɧ or ʂ — sound, in *sjuk*, *sju* and *sjutton* (spelled *sj*, *sk* and sometimes *ch* or *g*) is comparable to the Scottish *ch* in 'loch'. You may also feel confused about the three extra letters in the Swedish alphabet, and wonder what to do with erratic dots and rings above *a* and *o*. But bear in mind that what seems difficult to you is not necessarily important, and just because a word, letter or a sound appears familiar (and therefore easy to pronounce), this doesn't mean you pronounce it correctly. Letters and letter combinations that look commonplace to you may be pronounced completely different, as we are dealing with uniquely Swedish sounds.

However, for the curious learner, the most important thing to have in mind when learning how to pronounce Swedish is, in fact, not the individual sounds, but stress. In each word, one or two syllables are stressed, that is, prolonged in time. Either the vowel or the consonant in that syllable is significantly longer than the other syllables or sounds in the same word. This gives a rhythm to the language, making it intelligible for native speakers. If you fail to get the stress right, Swedish speakers will struggle to understand you, whereas they will still understand what you mean if some individual sounds are off.

For example, *fika* is pronounced with a long *i* sound, similar — but not identical — to the English E in 'see': *fiiiiika*. The stress is on the first syllable, and this is marked with a long vowel. *Kaffe* ('coffee') also has the stress on the first syllable, but in this case, the consonant (*f*) is long: *kafffffe*. In the word *kafé* (the small restaurant where you can buy your coffee) on the other hand, we put the stress on the second syllable, making a long *e*: *kafeeeee*.

As we mentioned earlier, this book comes without any pressure; no one is expecting you to speak fluent Swedish after reading it, but if you are curious to learn and have the ambition of making yourself understood in the company of Swedes, do focus on stress and don't worry so much about the individual sounds.

In the IPA pronuncation guides in this book, stress is marked with the symbol ː. This means that the preceding vowel or consonant is long:

fika	fiːka	ː after *i* means a long *i* sound: *fi<u>iiii</u>ka*
kaffe	kafːɛ	ː after *f* means a long *f* sound: *ka<u>fffff</u>e*
kafé	kafeː	ː after *e* gives a long *e* sound: *kaf<u>eeeee</u>*
choklad	ɧʊklɑːd	a long *a* in the Swedish word for chocolate, *chokl<u>aaaaa</u>d*
kanelbulle	kaneːlbɵlːɛ	in compound words, there are two stressed syllables, in this case a long *e* and a long *l* sound: *kan<u>eeeee</u>lbu<u>lllll</u>e*
prinsesstårta	prɪnsɛsːtoːʈa	again, two long syllables in compound words: *prinse<u>sssss</u>t<u>ååååå</u>rta*

If you want to learn more about the IPA and what Swedish sounds there are for you to master, have a look at the end of this book where they are listed. If it seems too technical to you, stick to the audio files or simply enjoy the words in their written — or even baked — form. Swedish pastries don't care about how you pronounce them, they are still just as tasty.

A 'Yes'; 'right'; 'I see'; 'I disagree' INTERJECTION

ɑː

This is a book about language, but the first thing you need to know is that the Swedes are often people of few words.

It's a stereotype, but one with roots in reality, that people in Sweden generally fall on the reserved or introverted side of the spectrum. Animated voices or gestures are less common than in many countries, particularly in formal contexts like at the office or among people you don't know well.

The Swedish word *ja* ('yes') is often pronounced 'ah', sometimes with the word almost inhaled so that it sounds like a gasp.

When pronounced this way, it can mean 'yes', but it's generally weaker than a spoken *ja*. It can also be a filler word — meaning 'I see', 'I understand', 'I'm listening', 'I'm not really listening so I'm making this noise instead of replying' or 'I disagree in the strongest terms, but I'm not going to say so'.

You'll have to use your intuition and rely on contextual cues!

- Vi har skrivit en bok.
- A...
- Den handlar om ord som har att göra med Sverige och svenskan.
- A...
***- Det första ordet är* a.**
- A...
***- Och sedan kommer* realisationsvinstbeskattning.**
- Va?

- We have written a book.
- OK.
- It's about words related to Sweden and the Swedish language.
- Right.
- The first word is *a*.
- I see.
- And then we have *realisationsvinstbeskattning*.
- What?

The shortest and the longest words

In Swedish, there are several words consisting of one letter only:

A — short for *ja*
E — sometimes used instead of *är* (am/are/is)
I — in
Å — a river or stream
Ö — an island

The first two are part of spoken or informal Swedish, but you will also see them in writing, especially in contexts like social media posts. *I*, *å* and *ö* are all words you can find in a dictionary and in books, news articles and so on.

According to the *Swedish Academy Dictionary*, the longest word in Swedish is:

realisationsvinstbeskattning
capital gains taxation

According to the *Guinness Book of World Records*, the longest word in Swedish is:

Nordöstersjökustartilleriflygspaningssimulatoranläggnings-materielunderhållsuppföljningssystemdiskusionsinläggs-förberedelsearbeten

which can be broken up to

nord-öster-sjö-kust-artilleri-flyg-spanings-simulator-anläggnings-materiel-underhålls-uppföljnings-system-diskussions-inläggs-förberedelse-arbeten

in English

North Baltic sea coast artillery aerial observation simulator facility equipment maintenance monitoring system discussion comment preparation work

which would (probably) mean

preparatory work for curating discussion points in the maintenance monitoring system for a simulator for aerial observation of the coast of the North Baltic Sea

AW 'After-work drinks or activity' NOUN

ɑːveː

This is an example of 'Swenglish' (or *svengelska*) — a mixture of Swedish and English.

In English, 'after-work' exists as an adjective, and it's either written as two separate words or hyphenated, since English speakers don't use compound words quite as often as Swedes. You can invite someone to go out for 'after-work drinks' or perhaps an 'after-work gym session' or you might talk in general about your 'after-work plans'.

In Swedish, *afterwork* is a noun referring to meeting up for drinks, usually alcoholic, after the working day. It's often shortened to *AW*, so you might see an *AW-meny* ('after-work menu') with happy-hour prices. Please note that Swedes make no distinction between the sounds *W* and *V*, which affects the pronunciation of Swenglish words.

There is an increasing tendency to use English words or phrases in (usually informal, spoken) Swedish. Often this happens with short phrases inserted into a Swedish sentence, for emphasis, like 'oh my God', 'no way', or 'best day ever', but some words like *afterwork* and *AW* have become part of the Swedish lexicon in their own right.

A similar word is *afterski*, the Swedish word for drinks after a day of skiing. Swedes use the English even if English speakers themselves tend to use the French term, *après-ski*.

Hänger du med på AW?
Are you coming to the drinks after work?

Någon som känner för en AW?
Is anyone up for after-work drinks?

Improve your Swenglish

Swedish has adapted some words from English, which are pronounced and spelled in a way familiar to English speakers but mean something different from what you might expect:

SWEDISH	ENGLISH
afterwork/AW	drinks with colleagues
babysitter	baby bouncer seat
blinkers	indicators (car)
dejt	romantic date
freestyle	walkman
kickoff	corporate event after summer
overall	snowsuit
playback	lip sync
pocket	paperback (book)
weekend	weekend break

Badkruka 'Someone who doesn't like swimming'

NOUN

baːdkrʉːka

This is the kind of insult you really only get here in Scandinavia.

A *badkruka* is someone who dislikes or refuses to swim, usually in an open body of water due to the low temperature of said water.

As you might have noticed if you've ever spent the summer in Sweden, many people spend a large portion of the season outdoors and engaged in active pursuits: hiking, climbing, and swimming.

These activities are typically done based on the time of year rather than the weather, so you'll find many Swedes leaping into extremely cold water just because "it's summer". *Badkruka* is a good-natured insult aimed at those who refuse to join them.

The word comes from *bada* ('to swim' — it shares roots with the English verb 'to bathe') and *kruka*, which literally means 'pot' or 'jug' but is also a slang term for 'coward'. So you could translate it as 'bathing coward'. *Kruka* in this sense comes from a dialect word meaning 'to bend over/crouch'.

Hoppa i, badkruka!

Jump in, scaredy-cat!

Björntjänst 'An action that has good intentions but negative consequences' NOUN

bjœːɳɐɛnːst

Björntjänst can be broken down into two words you might know fairly early on in your Swedish-learning journey.

Björn means 'bear'. The word has existed in almost the exact same form for centuries, probably coming from an older word for 'brown'.

Then we have *tjänst*, which means 'service' and is used in a wide variety of contexts. A company or an app might offer various *tjänster*; *kundtjänst* is 'customer services', and a *tjänsteperson* (literally 'service person') is a category of professionals, which originally meant those who provide services rather than products but these days usually refers to professions requiring tertiary education.

So what about *björntjänst*?

It comes from a 17th-century fairy tale, *The Bear and the Gardener* by Jean de La Fontaine (the story itself probably has even older origins). In the story, a gardener befriends a bear, and entrusts the animal with several tasks including keeping flies away from the gardener while he takes his nap (*tupplur*). All is going well until one especially persistent fly appears. The bear tries to crush it using a paving stone, killing the fly, but also the gardener. *Hoppsan* ('oops'), as the Swedes would say.

In the Swedish translation, the final line of this slightly bleak story is: *Även om motivet är ädelt, vill man helst slippa en björntjänst!* ('Even if the motive is lofty, it's always best to avoid a bear service!').

So a *björntjänst* is a well-meaning action that has negative or even disastrous consequences. There's an equivalent term in Russian (*medvezhya usluga*) and German (*der Bärendienst*), and the French expression *le pavé de l'ours* ('the bear's paving stone') refers to the same thing.

But many Swedes aren't aware of this backstory, so you might hear *björntjänst* used in different contexts today.

It might be used in the sense of 'a disservice' without the implication that the motives were good (in Swedish a more accurate word would be *otjänst*), or it may even be misused to mean something like 'a big favour' by people who think the word *björn* is being used for emphasis.

For example, in 2015, the local council in the town of Jönköping put up posters to advertise electric bikes and hybrid cars, using the slogan "*Gör både dig och miljön en björntjänst*" ("Do both yourself and the environment a favour that backfires"). You could even say that by creating these posters, the council did themselves a *björntjänst*.

Vi får inte göra vårt land en björntjänst.
We don't want to do our country a [well-intended] disservice.

Att prata engelska med nyanlända som vill lära sig svenska är att göra dem en björntjänst.
Speaking English with new arrivals who want to learn Swedish is a well-intended action with negative consequences.

Bear services and sun cats

Swedish is the language for you if you enjoy creative expressions with animals, referring to the human world:

björntjänst **'bear service'**
a favour that backfires

lipsill **'cry herring'**
crybaby

finansvalp **'finance puppy'**
a young and successful banking or finance professional

What do you think these expressions are referring to? Choose from the explanations below.

ankdamm	**'duck pond'**
dammråtta	**'dust rat'**
hundgöra	**'dog doings'**
snuskhummer	**'filth lobster'**
solkatt	**'sun cat'**
landkrabba	**'land crab'**

hard work dirty old man dust bunny
someone avoiding swimming or going on boats
a small and non-diverse group of people taking decisions
the reflection of the sun from a moving object, e.g. a watch

ankdamm = a small and non-diverse group of people taking decisions ◊ *dammråtta* = dust bunny ◊ *hundgöra* = hard work ◊ *snuskhummer* = dirty old man ◊ *solkatt* = the reflection of the sun from a moving object, such as a watch ◊ *landkrabba* = someone avoiding swimming or going on boats

Bostadsrättsförening 'Tenant owners' housing cooperative' NOUN

bu:stasrɛtsfœre:nɪŋ

The thing about buying an apartment in Sweden is that you don't actually buy the apartment. The key to understanding this is in one word: *bostadsrättsförening*.

Bostadsrättsförening can be broken down into *bostad* ('home' or 'property'), *rätt* ('right') and *förening* ('association').

A *bostadsrätt* means the right to live in a property, which is almost always what you buy when you purchase an apartment in Sweden.

You also buy into a collective, the *bostadsrättsförening*, which is the association in charge of running the property. This is most often one or several blocks of apartments, but it can also apply to groups of houses, especially terraced houses.

An English translation would be 'tenants' association' or 'housing cooperative'. Before you can move into a newly bought apartment, you need to be accepted by this cooperative, although this is usually just a formality.

Each month, as well as your mortgage, you'll pay fees to the *bostadsrättsförening*, often shortened to *BRF*. These fees cover maintenance of common areas like staircases, elevators and the communal laundry room, as well as things like plumbing, upkeep of external doors and windows, and often heating and water.

Some *bostadsrättsföreningar* offer extra perks such as a shared gym, sauna, or guest apartments for when members have visitors staying. In the plushest of *BRFs*, there might even be something like a pool or cinema just for residents.

The *BRF* sets rules for members, with the idea being that this ensures everyone can live comfortably. These rules typically include things like no loud noise after 10pm, and no smoking in common indoor areas.

So who are these mysterious people in charge? The *bostadsrättsförening* is made up of tenants living in the building, who take on roles on the *BRF*'s board and make decisions on how to use the money. Everyone living in the *BRF* gets a say, though, not just those on the board. There's no goal of making profit, so any extra money should be put back into benefits for *BRF* members.

Trevligt område, stabil bostadsrättsförening med bra ekonomi.
Pleasant neighbourhood, stable housing cooperative with good finances.*

Det är viktigt att analysera bostadsrättsföreningens ekonomi innan man köper lägenhet.
It is important to analyse a housing cooperative's finances before buying an apartment.

* You'll see phrases like this in estate agent adverts.

Brittsommar 'Indian summer' NOUN

brɪtːsɔmːaɾ

Brittsommar is the Swedish word for a late period of warm weather. In English you might call it an 'Indian summer', and the term *indiansommar* also exists in Swedish. In German-speaking countries, it's called *Altweibersommer* which would literally translate as 'old woman summer'.

What all three terms have in common is they don't mean what you might think: Indian summers aren't linked to India, *Altweibersommer* comes from an old word relating to cobwebs rather than old women, and *brittsommar* doesn't have any link to Great Britain. It literally means 'Britt summer', after Saint Bridget of Sweden, the only Swedish saint to have been canonised. The Swedish version of Bridget is *Birgitta*, sometimes shortened to *Britt*, and she has her saint day on October 7th.

You use the term to describe any period of warm weather in early autumn, if it comes after a cool spell. It's not a technical term; there is no specific date or temperature requirement.

But what's it got to do with Birgitta? It's not just about the timing of her national day. According to the meteorologists at Swedish weather agency *SMHI*, she wasn't a fan of the cold Nordic winters and prayed for warmer weather, so extra days of sunshine around her saint day are seen as an answer to these prayers.

SMHI says that a period of distinct warm weather in early October is rare in Sweden, but has happened in 1973, 1995, 2005 and 2018.

In older Swedish, the term *grävlingssommar*, literally meaning 'badger summer', was used to describe a late period of warmth, because badgers are active around this time collecting supplies for the winter.

Blir det någon brittsommar i år?
Will there be an Indian summer this year?

Brittsommar på väg in över Sverige.*
Late summer weather on its way to Sweden.

---

* This type of sentence, missing a verb, is typical of newspaper headlines.

Dagis 'Daycare' NOUN

dɑːgɪs

Dagis is an important word for families in Sweden. It's a colloquial term that refers to structured childcare for children aged between one and six, before their time at *förskoleklass* ('preschool class', a halfway stage between preschool and primary school) begins in August the same calendar year the child turns six.

Dagis is short for *daghem* ('day home' or 'home for the day') although the official name is actually *förskola* ('preschool').

In most larger Swedish towns and cities, it's possible to find international *förskolor*, and there are a few different types of *förskolor* so that parents can choose the one that best suits them in terms of location and activities.

In Sweden a very high proportion of youngsters attend *förskola*, partly because it's heavily subsidised and cheap for parents.

Municipalities are legally responsible for providing preschool care at *förskola*, and the system has existed in Sweden in some form since the early 1800s, when daycare was usually run by religious institutions.

However, it was only in 1943 that parliament decided on the names *daghem* and *lekskola* (literally 'playschool') as alternatives to the older name *barnträdgård* (literally 'child garden'), which was influenced by the German *Kindergarten*. The name *förskola* came a few years later, and was intended to emphasise the educational aspect of the centres. These days *lekskola* sounds quite old-fashioned but you'll still hear *dagis* used a lot.

Although more and more people use the official term *förskola* when talking about childcare, the term *dagis* is here to stay in other contexts. Homeware shop *Clas Ohlson* is sometimes jokingly referred to as *gubbdagis* ('daycare for older men') because of the stereotype that women might drop their husbands off there before continuing with their own shopping. That's slightly outdated now, after the company's CEO committed to improving gender equality in the business, and the store's customers are around 50 percent female.

Finally, dog owners should be aware of *hunddagis* ('doggy daycare'), which are common in Swedish cities due to strict laws about how long owners can leave dogs home alone.

Jag måste hämta min vovve på dagis.
I need to fetch my dog from daycare.

Jag älskar att gå på gubbdagis.
I love visiting homeware shops.

*En poppis skådis som är bakis**

In colloquial speech, Swedes often use a shortened version of the word with -*is* added as a suffix.

bakis *bakfull*	**hungover** 'back drunk'
godis *godsaker*	**sweets/candy** 'tasty things'
käftis *käft*	**dentist** 'mouth of an animal'
kändis *känd person*	**celebrity** 'known/well-known person'
loppis *loppmarknad*	**flea market** 'flea market'
mellis *mellanmål*	**afternoon snack** 'middle meal'
skådis *skådespelare*	**actor/actress** 'actor/actress'

* A popular actor who is hungover

If you look closely, many Swedish *is*-words share their etymology with English words that mean the same or something similar. Are you able to match the following Swedish words with their English translation?

1.	*kompis*	a.	best friend
2.	*grattis*	b.	ping pong
3.	*bäbis*	c.	companion
4.	*pingis*	d.	congratulations
5.	*poppis*	e.	baby
6.	*bästis*	f.	popular

kompis = friend (companion) ◊ *grattis* = happy birthday/congratulations (congratulations) ◊ *bäbis* = baby ◊ *pingis* = ping pong ◊ *poppis* = popular ◊ *bästis* = best friend

Dammsugare 'Vacuum cleaner' or 'marzipan pastry'

NOUN

dam:sʉ:garɛ

Here's a Swedish word that has two meanings, one useful and one delicious.

Dammsugare means 'dust-sucker', and it's the very literal Swedish name for a vacuum cleaner.

But more excitingly, it's also the name of a small Swedish pastry.

You'll find them at any traditional cafe in Sweden: green marzipan cylinders with their ends dipped in chocolate.

The official name is *punschrulle* ('punch roll') thanks to the liqueur that flavours the filling, but they're known as *dammsugare* or 'vacuum cleaners' for two reasons.

Firstly, they look similar to a model of vacuum cleaner that used to be popular in Sweden around the early 20th century. Perhaps that's one reason they're so beloved here, a kind of nostalgia.

Secondly, these treats are typically made using leftover biscuit crumbs for the filling — picture the baker vacuuming up these crumbs to repackage them in a brightly coloured *dammsugare*.

One story is that they were invented or at least became mainstream in the postwar period when ingredients for cakes were in short supply. Using crushed-up leftovers from unsellable biscuits meant bakers and buyers didn't have to use extra rations, while the liqueur and chocolate added a hit of flavour to the day-old crumbs. It's likely the extravagant marzipan topping was added later.

You'll find very similar cakes across northern Europe, known as 'tree trunks' in Denmark (where they don't usually contain liqueur) and 'little marrow bones' in the Netherlands. Three distinctly unappetising names for a popular snack.

Like many cakes and pastries in Sweden, the *dammsugare* has an 'official' day of celebration: March 7th. But they'll appear on the *fika* spread all year round, and now you know their story.

Other desserts with their own day on the calendar include Waffle Day on March 25th, Cinnamon Bun Day on October 4th, and Chocolate Cake Day on November 7th. Some of these dates have their roots in older, often religious celebrations, while others are mostly a marketing ploy.

Oj, jag har ätit för många dammsugare!
Oh no, I've eaten too many *dammsugare* cakes!

Jag behöver en dammsugare.
Either: 'I need a vacuum cleaner' or 'I need a *dammsugare* cake'.

Deckare 'Crime fiction' NOUN

dɛk:arɛ

As you may have noticed, Sweden has a strong tradition in detective fiction.

Deckare usually refers to books, but a TV series or film can also be a *deckare*. A similar English word would be 'whodunnit'.

The term comes from a shortening of *detektiv* (you probably don't need to be a 'detective' to work out that that's the English translation), since the protagonist in these stories is often a private detective. But books featuring a police officer, journalist, or a mystery solver of another profession can also fall under this heading.

One of the key defining features of the *deckare* is that the reader must have the same chance as the detective to solve the murder, meaning that all clues should be clear to readers as well as characters.

Deckare (the plural form is the same as the singular) have boomed in popularity over the past few decades, making up an increasingly large proportion of the bestseller lists in Sweden.

Du har läst för många deckare.
You've been reading too many detective novels.

Henning Mankell har skrivit flera deckare.
Henning Mankell has written several detective novels.

Dopp 'Dip' NOUN

dɔpː

*D*opp is similar to the English word 'dip' in the sense of taking a quick swim. For example: *Ska vi ta ett dopp?* ('Shall we go for a dip?').

The image of 'dipping' oneself in the water suggests more of a spontaneous, brief swim compared to using the verb *bada* ('to bathe') or *simma* ('to swim').

Simma is usually swimming with a purpose, for example if you're going from a shoreline to an island or doing laps in a pool, while *bada* is swimming for leisure, often with no clear destination.

Bada also implies spending a longer time in the water, while *ett dopp* can be used even if you just jump in and get straight back out. So in some places, the water might not be warm enough to *bada*, but it's perfect for *ett dopp*.

Going for a dip in your nearest lake or sea is a Swedish summer tradition, so a common question you can use in small talk over summer is *Har du tagit årets första dopp än?* ('Have you been for your first dip of the year yet?').

You can use compound words such as *morgondopp* ('morning dip'), *kvällsdopp* ('evening dip'), *semesterdopp* ('holiday dip'), and so on.

As in English, you can also use the word *doppa* ('to dip'

or 'to dunk') to talk about submerging something in liquid temporarily.

It appears in two fairly old-fashioned terms for Swedish food. *Kaffe med dopp* ('coffee with dip') is quite an outdated way of referring to a coffee and a biscuit, pastry or *smörgås* ('open sandwich').

Dopp i grytan (literally 'dip in the stew') is a traditional Christmas dish, made up of bread dunked in pork broth.

Jag kanske tar ett dopp idag.
I might take a dip today.

Jag var i vattnet men försökte att inte doppa håret.
I was in the water but tried not to get my hair wet/dip my hair in.

A fine line between 'ugly' and 'drunk'

In Swedish, stress is marked with a long syllable, either a long vowel or a long consonant. You may get some clues from the spelling; a long vowel is usually followed by a single consonant (*dop, ful, glas*), whereas a long consonant sound is usually spelled with two consonants (*dopp, full, glass*).

One letter can make a whole difference. A *fulgubbe* is a dirty old man, whereas a *fullgubbe* is an alcoholic.

There are plenty of minimal pairs, that is, two words that seem to be very similar but mean something completely different. Listen to the audio file to see if you can hear the difference between the word pairs. Long sounds are underscored.

dop	baptism/christening
dopp	dip/quick swim
ful	ugly
full	drunk
glas	glass
glass	ice cream
tak	roof/ceiling
tack	thank you
granar	Christmas trees
grannar	neighbours
Polen	Poland
pollen	pollen

Dricks 'Tip' NOUN

drɪk:s

Dricks means 'tip', as in the extra money you give to some service workers beyond the bill.

It's a shortening of *drickspengar* (you'll almost never hear this longer form), which is similar to the German term, *das Trinkgeld*. You can use it as a verb too: *dricksa* ('to tip').

It's related to the noun *dryck* ('a drink') and the verb *dricka* ('to drink') and according to the late Swedish etiquette expert Magdalena Ribbing, it has its origin in the custom of giving a small amount of money to a service worker so they can buy a drink for themselves.

Sweden's tourism board says it is "unlikely anyone will be offended" if you don't tip, but if you want to, it recommends tipping five to ten percent of the total bill or simply rounding up to an even sum, for example by paying 400 *kronor* if the bill is 380. It is generally not considered necessary to tip in Sweden, but it's more common at more formal restaurants.

Two things to be aware of about tipping in Sweden are, firstly, that you can't be sure how the tips will be divided between staff, and secondly that several trade unions are against tips — they say that this erodes their bargaining power and that it's better for service staff to have higher wages and good working conditions than to rely on tips which may fluctuate.

Ska vi dricksa?
Shall we leave a tip?

Det är vanligast att lämna dricks på restaurang.
It is most common to tip at restaurants.

Duktig 'Capable'; 'conscientious' ADJECTIVE

dɵk:tɪ

This word is usually a compliment, but you need to pay attention to context if you want to avoid causing offence.

Duktig means 'skilled', 'capable', or 'hard-working'. You might see or hear phrases like *Oj, vad duktig du är!* ('Wow, how skilled you are!').

You can use it to describe someone's general behaviour, in the same way as you might say in English 'You're such a hard worker!' or (to a child) 'good girl/boy!'. But it usually refers to an action, either a job or a specific task.

It is often used before a noun to highlight that someone is skilled in a particular role or capacity, so you could say: *Hen är en duktig målvakt/författare/förälder* ('He/she is a good goalkeeper/author/parent').

Or you can combine it with the preposition *på* and a verb or noun to praise specific *duktighet* ('talent/skill'): *Vad duktig du är på att rita!* ('How good you are at drawing!'). As well as describing the person, you can talk about the *duktiga* things they've done: *Hon gjorde många duktiga saker* ('She did lots of good things'), or use it as an adverb by adding *t*: *Han spelade duktigt* ('He played well').

Duktig comes from the verb *duga*, which means 'to be good for' or 'to be acceptable for'.

But the word is not without controversy. Some people argue that *duktig* can be patronising when used about an adult, since it is most often associated with parents or teachers talking to children (or even pet owners talking to their dogs), rather than peer-to-peer conversations.

With that said, if someone tells you you're *jätteduktig på svenska*, it is in all likelihood a sincere compliment.

Duktig hund!
Good dog!

De vill locka duktig personal till företaget.
They want to attract capable staff to the company.

Eller hur? 'Right?' PHRASE

ɛlɛhʉːɾ

Eller hur literally means 'or how'.

It's used at the end of a sentence and is roughly equivalent to saying 'right?', or 'isn't it?/doesn't it?/don't you think?' — basically you're seeking confirmation from the listener. But when you use *eller hur?* you're almost always expecting agreement.

If you're genuinely wondering if what you said is correct, you should add *eller?* ('or') to the end of your statement, but in this case, you would usually change the word order of your statement, just like in a normal question.

Compare the two sentences: *Tycker alla om kaffe, eller?* ('Does everyone like coffee, or...?') and *Alla tycker om kaffe, eller hur?* ('Everyone likes coffee, am I right?').

The first example is a genuine question, so someone might respond *Nja, jag dricker hellre te* ('Well, I prefer tea'). You could simply ask *Tycker alla om kaffe?* ('Does everyone like coffee?') but adding *eller?* makes it clear you really want a response. The second example is a rhetorical question.

An alternative to *eller hur?* is *inte sant?* (literally 'not true?').

You can add either of these two phrases to any statement to turn it into a question, without needing to change the word order or verb conjugation, the same way you can add 'right?' or 'correct?' to statements in English.

You can also use *eller hur* on its own as an emphatic response, expressing your agreement. For example, if someone says *Det är så gott med kanelbullar!* ('Cinnamon buns are so tasty!'), you can reply *eller hur?!* ('right?!'). This sounds much more colloquial and natural than some other grammatically correct responses, like *Ja, absolut!* ('Yes, absolutely!').

- Vi borde åka på semester tillsammans.
- Kanonidé!
- Eller hur?!
- We should go on holiday together.
- Great idea!
- Right?!

- Det var en jättebra film.
- Eller hur!
- That was a great film.
- It was, wasn't it!

Fettisdagen 'Shrove Tuesday' NOUN

fe:ti:sdan

Fettisdagen means 'fat Tuesday' (*fet* + *tisdag*), and it is the Swedish name for the Catholic celebration of Shrove Tuesday or Mardi Gras, being a literal translation of the latter. It takes place 47 days before Easter, in February or early March.

In Catholic tradition, this is the final day of Shrovetide, the period of confession and reflection before Lent, forty days of fasting or abstinence from luxuries. People would also use the final day before fasting to indulge in rich foods, hence the 'fat'.

In Sweden, which is predominantly secular, the day has mostly lost its religious connotations, and it's not a public holiday.

But the Swedes are not likely to pass up an opportunity to enjoy baked goods.

So the food-related part of the tradition has stuck around, and to most people in the country *fettisdagen* is simply a chance to eat *semlor*: wheat, cardamom-spiced buns filled with almond paste and lots of whipped cream.

In fact, the day is sometimes referred to as *semmeldagen* or *semlans dag*, while alternative names for the *semla* bun are *fettisdagsbulle* (literally a 'Fat Tuesday pastry') or *fastlagsbulle* ('Shrovetide pastry').

There's another name for the *semla*, *hetvägg*, used when it's eaten in a bowl of hot milk, a custom still practised around Sweden by some.

Många svenskar äter minst en semla på fettisdagen.
Many Swedes eat at least one *semla* on Shrove Tuesday.

Snart är det fettisdag.
Shrove Tuesday will soon be here.

Fredagsmys 'Friday cosiness' NOUN

fɾeːdasmyːs

*F*redagsmys is how Swedes typically celebrate the end of the working week. Think blankets and snacks at home rather than cocktails out on the town.

Fredagsmys means getting cosy on the sofa with some easily-prepared food (often tacos or pizza, fizzy drinks, crisps and sweets) and watching TV. There's usually another person involved: you can *mysa* with a partner, family, friends, or pets.

Mys is related to the adjective *mysig* ('cosy') and the verb *att mysa*, which can mean 'to cuddle/snuggle' but is also used more generally to mean 'to have a pleasant, relaxing, chilled-out time'. *Mys* is the Swedish equivalent of the Danish word *hygge*.

There are plenty of different varieties of *mys*: *höstmys*, *julmys*, *tacomys*, *kvällsmys*, *strandmys* ('autumn cosy time', 'Christmas cosy time', 'chilling out with tacos', 'being cosy in the evening', 'chilling out on the beach') and so on. But *fredagsmys* is one of the most commonly used forms.

It was most likely coined in the 1990s to describe an evening spent relaxing at the end of the five-day working week, first appearing in Swedish media in 1994 and entering the Swedish Academy's dictionary 12 years later. It was popularised by a TV advert for crisp brand *OLW*, which celebrated the concept of *fredagsmys* with a catchy jingle. There are equivalents in Norway (*fredagskos*) and Denmark (*fredagshygge*).

Order and routine are a big part of Swedish culture: pea soup is traditionally eaten on Thursdays, and sweets on Saturdays (known as *lördagsgodis* or 'Saturday sweets'). So it's only natural that their weekly downtime should be given a designated day too, and it highlights the value given to a healthy work-life balance.

You could even describe something (a film or recipe) as *fredagsmysig* or use the verb *fredagsmysa* (to have a cosy Friday night in).

Nu är det slut på veckan, det är dags för fredagsmys.
Now it's the end of the week, it's time for a cosy Friday night.

Jag älskar att fredagsmysa.
I love having a cosy Friday night in.

Funkis 'The style of residential properties built in the first half of the 20th century' NOUN

fəŋ:kɪs

This word is handy for property hunters or lovers of Swedish design.

Funkis is one of the many Swedish slang terms ending in *-is*. It comes from the longer term *funktionalism*, 'functionalism' in English. This is a specific architectural style which follows the principle that buildings should be designed with a focus on the intended function of the building, without ornate flourishes.

'Functionalism' could apply to offices and industrial buildings designed in the style, but when we use the shorter term *funkis*, it often refers to residential buildings. You might see phrases like *i funkisstil* (in functionalist style) or compound nouns such as *funkishus* and *funkislägenhet* (*funkis* building or apartment).

The 1930s were the main era of functionalism in Sweden, but many buildings in this style were also built before and after that decade.

They don't have grand, decorative facades like many earlier buildings, but instead are made mostly of rectangular or cube shapes, with big windows and balconies.

That doesn't mean they're boring or dreary, though. There was a focus on allowing plenty of light into each room, with *funkis* buildings designed to let in maximum sun at optimum times of day (for example in the kitchen in the mornings and in the living room, bedroom and balcony during the evening). They were mainly located in areas closely connected to town or city centres but with easy access to nature, a combination that still has great appeal today.

At the time they were built, these buildings were considered very forward-thinking because they included laundry rooms and rubbish disposal within the apartment blocks, and a bathroom in every apartment, which wasn't standard for the era. Because of that, they were also sometimes called *hygienhus* or 'hygienic buildings'.

Funkis buildings can be found in most towns and cities across the country, often clustered in the younger suburbs. They remain extremely popular among Swedes partly for their traditional character and partly because many still serve their function so well today.

Something else to be aware of: in recent years, *funkis* has also been used as shorthand for the term *funktionshindrad* (disabled). It's generally not considered pejorative, but as a non-native speaker it's best to exercise caution using slang terms where context is important.

En riktig funkispärla!
A real gem of the funkis style!*

Så inreder du din funkislägenhet.
Here's how to decorate your funkis apartment.

* An example of text you might find in a real estate brochure.

Fy 'Oh'; 'ew'; 'yuck'; 'bad (boy/girl/cat/dog)'

INTERJECTION

<u>fy:</u>

This is one of those words that may seem small and insignificant, but when deployed correctly can help you sound like a native Swede, however much of the language you know.

If a Swede starts a sentence with *fy*, brace yourselves, because it's a word that shows strong emotions.

You might hear it uttered alone — *Fy!* — but it usually comes before another word, often a swear word or another noun understood as a profanity.

Some common examples include *Fy bubblan!* ('Oh, the bubble!', roughly meaning 'my gosh!' — this one's quite safe to use), *Fy skäms!* ('shame on you/him/them' etc.), *Fy sjutton!* (literally 'Oh, seventeen!' — the number is often used as a tamer stand-in for more vulgar curses) or the most common, *Fy fan!* ('What the hell!', 'Holy shit!' or 'Fucking hell!').

Beware: you might hear the last example a lot, but only use it when you're absolutely sure it's an appropriate situation, because this is strong language. A milder option is *fy fabian*, which replaces *fan* in the same way English speakers might exclaim 'oh, sugar!' or 'fudge!' instead of swearing.

Although *fy* is nearly always negative, it may express surprise or emphasis in combination with other words.

In colloquial Swedish, *fy fan* can be used to show surprise or excitement, in a similar way to 'oh my God!' in English. For example *Fy fan, vad kul!* means 'Oh my God, how great!' and *Fy fan, vilken dag!* means 'Oh God, what a day!' but isn't necessarily negative — it may have just been a surprisingly busy or eventful day.

You'll also hear *fy* used a lot by pet owners; *Fy, Milo!* means something like 'Bad dog, Milo!'.

Fy has been around for centuries and existed in Old Norse too. And similar sounds are used to express disgust or anger in many languages. One of them is 'fie' in English, which has fallen out of use but was a popular interjection from the 13th century. English speakers may know it from the fairy tale *Jack and the Beanstalk*, in which a giant chants "fee-fi-fo-fum", or from Shakespeare plays like *King Lear*.

Å fy, vad äckligt!
Oh God, how disgusting!

Fy fan, vad gott!
Oh my God, how delicious.

Gift **'Married'; 'poison'** ADJECTIVE/NOUN

jɪfːt

'False friend' is the name given to words that look and sound like a word in another language but mean something completely different.

The Swedish word *gift* is a step beyond that: it has two distinct meanings in Swedish, neither of which is the same as the English 'gift'.

Gift means both 'married' (when used as an adjective) and 'poison' (when used as a noun).

It's not as strange as it might seem.

Both forms of *gift* have their roots in the Old Norse word *gipt*, which meant 'something given'. The meaning changed very little in English over the years, so the word 'gift' means 'present', but in Swedish, the word developed into *giva*, which became closely associated with marriage.

Years ago in Sweden, as in many other countries, marriage was seen as a transaction where the father 'gave' his daughter to her new husband. The word for 'dowry' was *hemgift*, and *gift* came to mean 'married'.

Today there is no negative or sexist connotation and it describes all married people, who are seen as equal partners in a marriage. In Swedish weddings, the marrying couple typically enter the church together to symbolise this equal partnership.

Meanwhile in Germany, the word *gipt* went on a very different etymological journey. Several centuries ago, *gift* was used to mean 'a present' but over the years the meaning changed until it became used solely as a euphemism for 'poison' somewhere around the year 800. Then, Sweden borrowed the noun *gift* ('poison') back from German, which is how we ended up with the two kinds of *gift*.

The key thing to remember is to check whether it's being used as an adjective or a noun.

To avoid confusion, it helps to learn the related words to each use of *gift*. The verb 'to marry' is *att gifta sig*, while the noun 'marriage' is *ett äktenskap* (and 'wedding' is *ett bröllop*).

In the sense of 'poison', the adjective 'poisonous' is *giftig* and the verb 'to poison (someone)' is *att förgifta (någon)*.

Thankfully, the Swedish word for 'a gift' is straightforward: *en present*.

Han är gift och har tre små barn.
He is married and has three small children.

Hon har tagit gift.
She has taken (consumed) poison.

Favourite false friends

False friends are words that seem to be the same in two languages, but actually have completely different meanings. Stay alert so that you don't mix up these words when speaking to a Swedish person.

bra *bh*	**good** bra
eventuellt *slutligen*	**maybe** eventually
fart *prutt*	**speed** fart
gift *present*	**married/poison** gift
kiss *puss*	**pee** kiss
leg *ben*	**ID** leg/bone
pigg *gris*	**alert/lively/perky** pig
semester *termin*	**holiday** semester
svimma *simma*	**to faint** to swim

Glögg 'Swedish mulled wine' NOUN

gl<u>œ</u>gː

It's fun to say, and more fun to drink. *Glögg* is heated wine, usually red although white varieties are available too, with spices, almonds and raisins added in. You'll also see alcohol-free versions, made with juice or non-alcoholic wine.

It's exceptionally popular, almost exclusively drunk around the Christmas season, when many Swedes host *glöggfester* ('mulled wine parties').

Swedes don't drink as much wine as some of their European neighbours, but wine is still the most popular alcoholic drink, and a significant proportion of that is mulled wine. Around five million litres of *glögg* are consumed in Sweden every year, most of it in December.

The pronunciation of *glögg* sounds ever so slightly like the noise you make while gulping down a mug of the stuff at a cold Christmas market, but the origin of the word is not onomatopoeic.

It comes from the Old Swedish word *glödga*. This word has its origins in the verb *glöda* ('to glow'), and meant something like 'to heat up until it glows'. Heated wine was popular even among the ancient Greeks and Romans, who also added spice to the concoction, very likely to counter impurities in the wine.

These days, *glödga* is still used in Swedish but has a narrower meaning, 'to mull'. Like the English verb, this can refer to warming drinks or to considering something and 'mulling it over' in one's mind.

The oldest written record of the word *glögg* is from the early 19th century, even though Swedes were warming up their wine in winter for centuries before that. Records of *glödgat vin* date back to the 1600s, and we know that Gustav Vasa, one of Sweden's most famous rulers in the early 1500s, drank wine heated up with honey, cinnamon, cardamom and ginger.

Swedish mulled wine, and with it the word *glögg*, has been exported to neighbouring countries, giving rise to the word *gløgg* in Denmark and *glögi* in Finland.

Glögg är en väldigt viktig dryck runt jul.
Glögg is a very important drink around Christmas.

Glögg dricks ur små koppar och serveras med mandel och russin eller pepparkakor.
Glögg is drunk from small cups and served with almonds and raisins or gingerbread.

Grym 'Cruel'; 'great' ADJECTIVE

grʏmː

Grym is used in two seemingly contradictory ways, one negative, one positive.

The negative sense, translated as 'cruel', 'heartless' or 'mean' is the original. *Grym*, like English 'grim', has its origins in an Old Norse word which referred to something fierce and savage. You might hear about *grym* treatment of someone or a *grym* tyrant.

But from the 1970s onwards, the word underwent a transformation.

Swedes began to use *grym* in a positive sense, meaning something like 'cool' and referring to people, objects or experiences. You can also use it to mean 'good' or 'great', in sentences like *Jag är grym på det* ('I'm good at that'). The change can be compared to the slang use of 'wicked' in English.

Generally, the original negative meaning is used in more serious contexts, such as political speeches, academic papers and non-fiction books. The newer, positive sense is popular among younger people in informal contexts, and in newspapers' sports and entertainment sections (but very rarely in news sections).

So, the sentence *han är grym* could refer to a brutal oppressor or to an attractive or cool man. You'll have to rely on other context to figure out which is intended.

Another thing to be aware of is that there's also an adverbial form of *grym*, *grymt*. This can be used as a form of negative *grym*, meaning 'cruelly' or 'savagely', but can also simply be used as an intensifier meaning 'really' or 'very', in sentences like *Det var grymt kul* ('It was really fun').

En grym och brutal död.
A cruel and brutal death.

Hon är grym på att springa.
She is great at running.

Gröt 'Porridge' NOUN

gɾøːt

Gröt means 'porridge', a warming food made from oats and water or milk and beloved in Sweden since Viking times.

There are many, many different kinds of *gröt* ranging from *trollgröt* or *klappgröt* (a lingonberry porridge eaten for dessert and whisked into a liquid), *nävgröt* (a substantial Värmland variant served with pork), *julgröt* (a dish similar to rice pudding and traditionally eaten on Christmas), which is also called *tomtegröt* (the porridge traditionally left out for the household gnome, similar to how families in some cultures leave out milk and snacks for Father Christmas), to many others.

A related word are *grötslev* or 'porridge ladle', a kitchen utensil specifically for the serving of porridge (usually made out of wood). Swedes are big fans of having specific tools for certain foods, with the cheese slicer and butter knife being two other examples.

The adjective *grötig* ('porridge-y, porridge-like') describes something thick and unclear, and perhaps muddled — look out for Swedes describing the Danish language as *grötigt.* Despite the popularity of porridge, this *grötig* is not a compliment. And *gröt* itself can be used in a metaphorical sense to mean 'mess' or 'muddle' or talk about something unclear.

Because porridge itself has existed in Sweden for centuries, the Swedish language has long had words for porridge: *grøter* in early varieties of Swedish and *grautr* in Old Norse before that.

These words have their origins in the even older word *greuna*, which meant something like 'to coarsely grind'. This is the root of other words such as *gryta* ('stew') and *grus* ('gravel/pebbles') in Swedish too, but these were much more recent additions to the vocabulary than *gröt*.

Gröt also pops up in some Swedish idioms and proverbs.

Het på gröten (literally 'hot on the porridge') is used to describe someone very eager about something or someone, often but not always with romantic or sexual connotations. For example: *Anna är het på gröten för Jonas* ('Anna is keen on Jonas').

Gå som katten kring het gröt (literally 'to walk like the cat around hot porridge') is the Swedish equivalent of 'to beat around the bush', meaning to take a long time to get to the point. In fact, the English language has its own feline version: 'to pussyfoot around something'. So if you say *Hon gick inte som katten kring het gröt*, it means 'She got straight to the point'.

And if you describe someone as *grötmyndig*, it means 'haughty', 'pretentious' or 'loud-mouthed'. Although you could translate it literally as 'of an age to make porridge' or 'authoritative in matters of porridge', this word has a different, non-porridge-related origin. It comes from Low German *grootmündig*, which became *großmundig* in today's German and literally means 'big-mouthed'.

Gröt är god och nyttig mat.
Porridge is a tasty and healthy food.

Ska vi äta gröt till frukost?
Shall we have porridge for breakfast?

Gubbe & gumma 'Old man/boy' & 'old woman/girl' (slang) NOUN

gɵbːɛ gɵmːa

Gubbe is a word to describe men or boys, and *gumma* is the equivalent for women or girls. Both can be either affectionate or derogatory.

When talking to your friends about your grandfather, for example, you might refer to him as *gubben*; it's an endearing way of saying 'old man'.

You can use the terms *lilla gubben* and *lilla gumman* (roughly 'little fellow' and 'little lady') as terms of affection for young children, or even pets. But *gubbe* and *gumma* can also be used as insults, so you need to be careful — especially when talking about someone you don't know.

A good example of how the meaning can change is when Swedish-speaking women use it to refer to their husbands.

When said in an affectionate context, *min gubbe* is a colloquial way of saying 'my husband', similar to the British 'my man' or 'my bloke', and usually no offence would be intended at all. However, it can be used to criticise men for letting themselves go: magazine articles on 'Signs your man has become a *gubbe*' might give criteria such as wearing old, worn out clothes, allowing nose and ear hair to grow, preferring to stay at home rather than go out, and growing grumpy.

If you really want to insult someone, *gubbe* can be coupled with adjectives such as *sur* ('sour/grumpy'), making *surgubbe* ('grumpy old man') or *ful gubbe* (literally 'ugly man' but used to mean 'dirty old man' or 'letch').

Gumma is mostly used to describe older women, but can also be affectionate or insulting, depending on the tone. So think twice before you call somebody a *gubbe* or *gumma* — it can come off harsher than intended and is almost never appropriate if you aren't close with the subject.

Swedish language learners might be wondering if there's any link to the word for strawberry: *en jordgubbe.*

The short answer: no. *Gubbe* is also a Swedish dialect word to refer to a small lump, and *jord* means 'earth' in the sense of soil, so a strawberry is quite simply 'a small lump that grows in the earth'. Most linguists believe that this dialect word was the origin of *gubbe* meaning 'man', probably first used to refer to small children. Over time, it's likely that it started being used more widely to men of all ages, but it might explain the sometimes negative connotations.

One final form of *gubbe* to watch out for: in Swedish slang, *en gubbe* also means a gram of drugs.

Min man har blivit en tråkig gubbe.
My husband has become a boring old man.

Jag gick på teater med gumman.
I went to the theatre with the wife.

Gärna 'Gladly' ADVERB

jæːɳa

Gärna is a very useful Swedish word. It can be literally translated as 'willingly' or 'gladly', but is used much more often and in more informal contexts than either of those words in English.

Speakers of other languages might spot the similarity with German *gern*, Danish *gerne* and Icelandic *gjarna*. All these words share a root in the Old Norse word *gjarn* ('willing' or 'eager').

So how do you use it? *Gärna* can be used as an adverb in sentences like *Jag tar gärna en kaffe* (literally 'I'll happily have a coffee' but closer to 'I'm happy to have a coffee/I'd like to have a coffee') or *Jag hjälper dig gärna* ('I'm happy to help you').

You can also use it on its own, in which case it's a snappier alternative to 'yes, I'd like that' or 'yes please!' For example:

-Vill du följa med? ('Would you like to come along?') *-Gärna!* ('I'd love to!')

- Vill du ha mjölk och socker? ('Do you want milk and sugar?') *-Gärna mjölk, tack* ('Milk, please')

Gärna can also be used when you're talking about someone else, such as in the sentence *Hon pratade gärna* ('She was happy to talk') or *Hon vill gärna följa med* ('She would like to come too').

It can also mean 'if you like', for example *Ta gärna kontakt* ('Feel free to get in touch' or 'Please get in touch') or *Ta gärna med hunden* ('Bring your dog if you like'). In these examples, *gärna* softens the requests: *Ta med hunden* ('Bring your dog') is a command, but adding *gärna* emphasises that the decision is up to the listener. This phrasing is particularly common in situations where the speaker is encouraging someone to do something they may think they aren't allowed to.

But you can also use *gärna* to phrase something as a command that isn't really optional, without being overly aggressive, especially when combined with the verb *få* ('ought/can'). Telling someone *du får gärna ta kontakt* could gently urge them to get in touch, or even be a slightly passive-aggressive reminder that they should already have been in touch.

Gärna can also be used when you're not implying any choice or pleasure linked to the action, but simply saying that something happens readily, easily, or often. This is common when talking about inanimate objects, for example *Den går gärna sönder* (literally 'It likes to fall apart' but actually meaning 'It falls apart easily').

Finally, the phrase *lika gärna* means something like 'just as easily' or 'just as well'. For example, *Det hade lika gärna kunnat vara jag* means 'It could just as easily have been me' and *Hon använde inte ordet "ful", men det hade hon lika gärna kunnat göra* means 'She didn't use the word "ugly", but she may just as well have done'.

Jag vill gärna träffa dig
I'd like to meet you.

Visst, gärna det.
Sure, I'd like that.

Halka 'Slippery walking/driving surface' NOUN

hal:ka

If you plan to drive or even walk along a Swedish winter road, *halka* is a word you need to know. There's no one-word English equivalent, but it describes icy weather conditions where there's a high chance of skidding.

There are several different kinds of *halka*.

Frosthalka appears when there's no snow, but moisture in the air freezes on the roads. It's most common during the autumn, after clear, cold nights.

In the winter, you get *snöhalka*, when fallen snow leaves the roads slippery.

But the most common and most dangerous phenomenon is *ishalka*, also called *blixthalka* or *svarthalka*. In English, this is called 'black ice' and it refers to times when there's a thin layer of ice on the roads, caused by rain or drizzle freezing when it falls on a surface below 0°C. It's transparent, but is called *svarthalka* because you can see the black asphalt through the clear ice.

Halka can also be used as a verb, meaning 'to slip/slide'. Unlike the noun, the verb *halka* doesn't need to have anything to do with ice or cold weather. It can also be used figuratively: *halka efter* means 'to fall or lag behind', or you might *halka* on something other than ice.

The idiom *halka in på ett bananskal* ('to slide in on a banana skin') is used to mean 'to end up doing something completely coincidentally/by accident'.

So you could say: *Jag hade aldrig tänkt att jag skulle bo i Sverige, jag halkade in på ett bananskal* ('I had never thought I would live in Sweden, I slipped in on a banana skin/it happened completely coincidentally').

SMHI varnar för halka.
SMHI [Sweden's weather agency] warns of slippery road conditions.

Vem som helst kan halka på vintern.
Anyone can slip [on ice] in the winter.

Hej **'Hello'** INTERJECTION

hɛjː

Hej, pronounced like English 'hey', is a Swedish greeting, an alternative to *hallå* ('hello') or *goddag* ('good day') although the latter is extremely formal and not used in everyday contexts.

Hej is the most common and safest of the three to use as a non-native speaker.

The word *hej* has existed in the Swedish language for centuries, but previously it was an interjection, appearing for emphasis in old poems and songs, while *hallå* and *goddag* were used for greetings. Things started to change in the 19th century when the Geatish Society, a group of Swedish writers with a fondness for antiquity, decided to adopt *hej* as their greeting because they liked its Old Norse feel, and it later became popular among students at Swedish universities.

Hej didn't really take off until the 1930s, and for a while it was a specifically informal greeting. When Sweden used different modes of formality when addressing people, *hej* was only used with people you called *du* ('you' that was used for people you were close with). But in recent decades the distinction between different forms of address has been eroded, so *hej* became more and more common and is now the most usual greeting in Swedish.

So how to use it?

You use it on its own in passing, *Hej!*, or at the start of a conversation, *Hej, hur mår du?* ('Hello, how are you?'). This also applies to emails, which are typically less formal than in English or many other languages — you'll sound much more natural and polite saying *Hej Benny!* than *Kära Herr Andersson* ('Dear Mr Andersson').

You can use more colloquial variations if you want.

In Swedish, it's common to double up words for emphasis, for example *tack tack* (literally 'thanks thanks') and *ja ja ja* ('yes yes yes'). So *hej hej* is more enthusiastic than a simple *hej*.

Another informal variant is to use the preposition *på*, for example *Hej på dig!* ('Hello to you [singular]!') or *Hej på er!* ('Hello to you [plural]!').

And there's the alternative *hejsan*, slightly more colloquial than *hej*. Again, this is more enthusiastic — a signal that you're in an upbeat mood and are talking to a friend.

The final thing to know about *hej* is that it's not exclusively used at the start of meetings. *Hej då* or simply *hej* is the Swedish term for 'bye'.

Hej på dig.
Hello.

Hej med dig.
Bye.

Helg **'Weekend'; 'holiday'** NOUN

hɛl:j

En helg means 'a weekend' in Swedish. You can also use the term *veckoslut*, (*vecka* — 'week', *slut* — 'end') literally meaning 'weekend', but *helg* is much more common.

I helgen means 'at the weekend' and can be used in both past and future tense, while *på helgen* means 'at the weekend' in present tense, to refer to something that happens every weekend.

You'll hear the phrase *trevlig helg!* '[have a] nice weekend!' when saying goodbye to people on a Friday. And it's incorporated into other words, such as *helgmat* ('weekend food'), *helgmys* ('weekend cosiness'), *helgutflykt* ('weekend trip') and so on.

The English term 'weekend' has been used in Sweden since the 1980s, but it has a slightly different meaning. When Swedes refer to *en weekend* rather than *en helg*, they mean an experience that's out of their usual routine, such as a trip away or a special experience.

Helg also refers to national holidays or festivals, including religious ones. It comes from the Old Norse *helgr* (plural *helgar*), the word for holy festival days which was related to the words *heilagr* ('holy') and *helga* ('to hallow').

Swedish has another word for national or religious holidays, *helgdag*, which has the same etymological roots as English 'holiday' and Norwegian/Danish *helligdag*. Danish, however, uses the term *weekend* to refer to Saturday and Sunday in order to keep a distinction between regular weekends and holidays, unlike Sweden which calls them both *helg*.

In Swedish, *helgdagar* are also called *röda dagar* ('red days') and include Christmas and Easter for example.

Around these special holidays, but particularly the Christmas and New Year period, you'll hear the greeting *God helg!* meaning roughly 'Happy holidays!' or 'Happy festive season!', as a secular alternative to *God jul!* ('Merry Christmas!'). Note the difference between *god helg* for holidays and *trevlig helg* for ordinary weekends.

Är det helg än?
Is it the weekend yet?

Vad har du gjort i helgen?
What did you do over the weekend?

Hemsk **'Terrible'** ADJECTIVE

hɛm:sk

The meaning of *hemsk* has changed a lot over the years. Today, the adjective *hemsk* means 'terrible', 'awful' or 'grim', so it has decidedly negative connotations. The noun *hemskhet* means 'horror'.

You can also add a *t* to use it as an adverb, *hemskt*, which is usually pronounced without the *k*.

As an adverb, it is similar to the English word 'terribly' and can be used as an intensifier without any negativity. For example, you could say *Filmen var hemskt bra* ('The film was awfully good'), or *Vi var hemskt kära!* ('We were terribly in love!').

The meaning of *hemsk* has changed over time: it has the word *hem* ('home') as its root and was originally used to describe things connected to the home.

Then it came to refer to people who had never left home, and gradually the meaning evolved to become 'timid', 'foolish' or 'dull'. This negative meaning was further strengthened over time until it came to mean 'terrible'.

During the 19th century, a well known Swedish poet, Elias Sehlstedt, wrote a poem called *Hemskt är lifvet* ('Life is ghastly'). It wasn't all doom and gloom though; he repeated the phrase *innan man blir van* ('before you get used to it') throughout.

If you do want to describe something as 'homey' in Swedish,

you probably want a word like *trivsam* ('comfortable/cosy'), *enkel* ('simple, unfussy') or *hemtrevlig* ('just like home, cosy').

Vilken hemsk tanke.
What a horrible thought.

Jag är hemskt ledsen.
I'm terribly sorry.

Hen 'They' (singular) PRONOUN

hɛnː

Hen is Sweden's gender-neutral personal pronoun, an alternative to *hon* ('she') and/or *han* ('he') when referring to a person of non-binary gender, or in a context where their gender is unknown or irrelevant. It means speakers or writers can avoid clunky phrasing like repeating *han eller hon* ('he or she') or *kunden/studenten* ('the customer/student').

An English-language equivalent is single-person 'they', and there's an even closer equivalent in Finnish: *hän*, which has been used in this way since the 16th century and even features in the earliest printed book in the language.

Swedish *hen* is a much newer creation and it didn't arrive without controversy.

Language professor Karl-Hampus Dahlstedt is the first person to be reported as using the word, as far back as the 1950s. But for the next generation, its usage was confined to small circles, particularly those which focused on LGBT issues and gender expression. The pronoun re-entered mainstream discourse only in 2012, when *Olika förlag*, a publishing company specialising in promoting 'non-traditional' stories, released the children's book *Kivi och monsterhund* ('Kivi and Monster Dog') by Jesper Lundqvist, which only used *hen* to refer to its characters.

Since then, linguistic records show that its use has soared, in books, news media, legal documents, and parliament. It officially entered the Swedish Academy's dictionary in 2015.

The Swedish language has undergone other significant changes in order to reflect those already taking place in society. The obvious example is the *du* reform of the 1960s, when Sweden overhauled its form of address.

Previously, the pronoun *du* (singular 'you') was used only to address children, siblings, and close friends, or in other extremely informal contexts with no status difference. Elsewhere, there was a rather complex system which involved referring to people in the third person and by their title. This meant saying things like 'I hope the manager has a nice weekend' or 'Please could the accountant send the documents over?' when speaking to the person in question, and using the titles *herr*, *fru* and *fröken* ('Mr', 'Mrs' and 'Miss') if the person's title or rank was unknown.

In the early 1900s, attempts were made to adopt *ni* (plural 'you') as the formal term of address in parallel to French *vous* (meaning both plural 'you' and formal singular 'you'), and German *Sie* (meaning formal 'you'). But this never quite took off, and many people instead interpreted *ni* as a rude implication that the addressee's rank was not important.

By the 1950s and 1960s, growing liberalisation provided the appropriate background for the change to *du*, which began with newspapers such as *Dagens Nyheter* adopting the term in their style guides, and was spurred along by high-profile figures using the term, not least Prime Minister Olof Palme who, after his appointment in 1969, asked reporters to address him as *du*.

These days the lack of formality in the language, and especially the use of first names and *du* even with managers, is something that strikes many newcomers to Sweden. It reflects — or perhaps even encourages — typically informal working cultures.

Language is an evolving organism, and it's defined by how people use it rather than any rules imposed from above. So it makes sense that in order for a language change to take root, it needs to reflect its society.

A study from researchers at Lund University in 2018 analysed Swedes' feelings about *hen*. Although the majority of people surveyed said they never used the pronoun, the survey showed that Swedes who lived in big cities, were aged under 26, and had a university education, were most positive towards *hen* and most likely to use it often.

Hen has its critics, who argue the pronoun is unnecessary or political. These are on average more likely to be older people who live in rural areas and have more conservative political views, according to the same study.

Idag kommer läkaren, säg till när hen är här.
The doctor is coming today, let me know when they are here.

Om en anställd blir sjuk ska hen informera chefen.
If an employee falls ill, they should inform the boss.

Husmanskost 'Traditional everyday food' NOUN

hʉ:smanskɔs:t

Husmanskost is tough to translate directly into English. It means something along the lines of 'traditional Swedish food', 'everyday food', or 'good, plain food'. Think simple meals based on ingredients readily available in Sweden: meatballs and mashed potatoes, reindeer or elk stews, simple fish recipes, and so on. It's the kind of food you can expect to be served at a classic, no-frills Swedish pub.

Key features of *husmanskost* are that the ingredients are fairly cheap, and the dishes are high in fat, because traditionally this food needed to sustain agricultural workers. Some of the most typical cooking methods are stewing and boiling, and spices are rarely added to the food. For extra flavour, you'll instead see lingonberries served with almost every dish.

You can use the term *husmanskost* to talk about other countries' traditional cuisines too: for example, *klassisk libanesisk husmanskost* means 'classic, traditional Lebanese food'.

Husman means 'house/property owner' (from *hus* — 'building/house' and *man* — 'man'). This referred to people living rurally, who owned just their home rather than any surrounding land. They ate very differently from wealthy upper classes who could employ cooks and afford more expensive ingredients.

Kost is an older word meaning 'diet' or 'fare'. Look out for it in compound words, such as *vegankost* ('a vegan diet'), *kosttillskott* ('dietary supplement'), or *råkost* ('raw food' or 'raw food diet').

So, *husmanskost* is old-fashioned and unfussy, traditionally eaten at home. But from the early 20th century onwards, even as Sweden underwent industrialisation, this type of food began to appear in taverns and inns, and it's still remarkably popular among locals and tourists alike. These days, the word *husmanskost* on a restaurant sign or menu is intended to indicate high quality, hand-cooked food.

And over the past few years some chefs and restaurants have reinvented or updated the classic dishes, creating what's been called *nouvel husman* ('new traditional Swedish food'). These dishes may include non-Swedish ingredients or spices, and may also reduce the butter or cream to be lower-fat.

Den här restaurangen serverar klassisk, vällagad svensk husmanskost – helt fantastiskt!
This restaurant serves classic, well-prepared traditional Swedish food – totally fantastic!

Jag skulle vilja lära mig laga svensk husmanskost.
I would like to learn to cook traditional Swedish food.

Foodie false friends

Food vocabulary are some of the most crucial words when learning a new language. But in Swedish there are a lot of 'false friends' in the kitchen, so watch out for these deceptive names when ordering a meal in Sweden, or chatting to Swedes about food.

biff	**steak**
nötkött	beef
chef	**boss**
kock	chef
full	**drunk**
mätt	full (after eating)
glass	**ice cream**
glas	glass
delikat	**delicious**
ömtålig	delicate
kummin	**caraway**
spiskummin	cumin
svamp	**mushroom**
träsk	swamp
vin	**wine**
ranka	vine
vispa	**whisk**
viska	whisper

Hörni **'You guys'** INTERJECTION

hœɳ : ɪ

Hörni can mean a few different things, but put simply, it's a way of getting the attention of a group of people.

Hörni comes from the verb *höra* ('to hear/listen') and the pronoun *ni* (plural 'you'). You could translate it literally as 'listen up, you!' but the meaning is closer to 'guys!' or 'hey!'. It can be spelled with either one *r* or two: *hörni* or *hörrni.*

You're most likely to hear it when one person is trying to get the attention of several others: perhaps a teacher in Swedish class ready to announce the next task, or when you're trying to get several people to pause their individual conversations to listen to you. For example:

Hörni, jag måste gå ('Right guys, I've got to go').

Hörni, jag måste berätta någonting för er ('Guys, I have to tell you something').

Hörni, vad sägs om en fika? ('Hey guys, what about a *fika*?').

You can follow it with a plural noun to be more specific about who your greeting is addressed to: *hörni tjejer* ('hey girls'), *hörni allihopa* ('hey everyone'), and so on.

And you can use it after a statement: *Tack för allt, hörni!* ('Thanks for everything, guys!'), *Glad midsommar, hörni!* ('Happy Midsummer, everyone/guys!') or *Jag älskar er, hörni!* ('I love you guys!').

Swedish also has the similar word *hörrdu*, which usually becomes *hörru* in speech and is used when speaking to only one person, for example *Hörru, Nils!* ('Hey, Nils!').

Hörni and *hörrdu* are features of informal, spoken Swedish. That doesn't mean you won't encounter them in written Swedish too, but in that case it tells you that the writer wants to make the tone more conversational.

Hörni, hörni, kan vi sluta nu?
Guys, guys, can we stop now?

Hörni, kan ni hjälpa till?
Guys, can you help out?

Höst 'Autumn' NOUN

hœs : t

Höst is the Swedish word for 'autumn' — not to be confused with *hosta* ('cough').

I höst means 'this autumn', which you say if you are talking about the upcoming autumn, or if the season has already begun. You use it with the future or present tense.

Jag ska gifta mig i höst ('I will get married this autumn').

I höstas means 'last autumn', and you use it to talk about the previous autumn, using the past tense.

Jag gifte mig i höstas ('I got married last autumn').

På hösten means 'in the autumn' and you use it to talk about autumn in general, usually with the present tense.

Jag vill gifta mig på hösten ('I want to get married in the autumn' [in general, no specific autumn]).

To talk about the autumn of a specific year, past or future, you can say *hösten* + year.

Jag gifte mig hösten 1993 ('I got married in the autumn of 1993').

In Sweden, the autumn season has a strict meteorological definition.

Höst only arrives once the average daytime temperature has stayed below an average of 10°C for five consecutive days. When that threshold is reached, the first day of the five-day period is considered the start of autumn. Autumn then becomes winter when the average temperature is below an average of 0°C for five consecutive days. That means *höst* arrives and lasts for very different times depending on where you are in the country.

Höst used to mean 'harvest', with both the Swedish and English words related to the Old Norse word *haust*. *Haust* originally referred to gathering, but became used as the general term for the season in which farmers gathered their crops.

In the UK, as populations moved away from rural living, *haust* was overtaken by 'autumn' from the Latin term *autumnus* in general speech, and from the 1500s onwards 'harvest' took on a narrower, specifically agricultural meaning.

But further north, rural farming societies lasted much longer and they and their languages were less influenced by Latin. So Sweden kept the word *höst*, related to German *der Herbst* and Norwegian *haust*. Today, the Swedish word for 'harvest' is *skörd*.

There are lots of compound words linked to *höst*, such as *höstmys* ('autumn cosiness') or *höstlov* ('autumn break').

And like in English, you can talk about *höst* figuratively to talk about a late stage in a process, for example *på livets höst* ('in the autumn of life'), a metaphorical way to refer to older age.

Det blir en tidig höst i år.
Autumn is coming early this year.

Jag kom till Sverige hösten 2018.
I came to Sweden in the autumn of 2018.

Höstrusk 'Nasty damp autumn weather' NOUN

hœs:trɵs:k

The Swedish pastime of complaining about the weather is so prevalent that it has its own word.

Höstrusk is about as Swedish as a word can get, and doesn't just describe an undesired autumnal weather condition, it also encompasses the mood and feeling that goes with it.

Höstrusk best translates as 'nasty damp autumn weather'. *Rusk* means nasty or horrible and is heavily used among Swedes in October and November to describe the rainy, cold, and grey period just after the trees lose their leaves but when it's still too early for snow and Christmas lights.

You'll also hear people talking about *regn och rusk*, 'rain and nasty dampness'.

The word has a negative ring to it and its application pretty much coincides with when the Swedes start spending much more time indoors (a period which generally lasts until the spring and has earned them the reputation of 'isolating' themselves during the winter months).

Swedish writer, poet and painter August Strindberg (1849–1912) doesn't seem to have been a big fan of the Swedish *höstrusk*. In 1885, he wrote that "All that was left for me to do was to go on a journey in the midst of *höstrusket*" ("*För mig återstod således blott att midt i höstrusket företaga en resa*").

Jag ger mig aldrig ut i det där höstrusket.
I'll never head out into that nasty autumn weather.

Njut av vädret innan höstrusket kommer.
Enjoy the weather before the nasty autumn weather sets in.

Regn och rusk

You find many expressions and phrases based on rhymes and alliterations in Swedish:

regn och rusk	**'rain and nasty weather'** bad weather
frid och fröjd	**'peace and joy'** all well

What do you think should be the second part of the following expressions? Choose from the list below.

nära och	near and dear ones
pick och	belongings
huller om	chaotic
ris och	positive and negative feedback
hipp som	without a plan (negative)
titt som	very often

buller happ kära pack ros tätt

nära och kära ◊ *pick och pack* ◊ *huller om buller* ◊ *ris och ros* ◊ *hipp som happ* ◊ *titt som tätt*

Jaha **'Oh really'; 'ah, right'** INTERJECTION

jaha:

This word will make you sound infinitely more Swedish, and can be used in almost any situation.

Jaha can mean 'really?', 'right then', 'so', 'oh', 'ah, right!' and many more things, depending on the context.

One common use is to show understanding of something, for example if someone says *Här på kontoret fikar vi tre gånger om dagen* ('We have *fika* three times a day in the office'), you could say *jaha* ('OK' or 'I see'). Or if someone explains something you've been puzzling over, you might say, *Jaha, så det var därför* ('Aha, so that's why').

You can indicate surprise, excitement, scepticism or any other emotion you want through the tone of your *jaha*. To emphasise surprise, an alternative response would be *Jaså!* which means something like 'Is that so?!'

You can also use *jaha* as a filler word to indicate a change of subject, or conclusion of something.

For example, if your group of friends has finished eating at a restaurant and paid the bill, and you're sitting waiting for someone to make the first move to leave, you can say *Jaha?* to indicate that you're ready. In this case, it's similar to 'Right then' or 'Shall we?' in English.

After a film has finished, or a conversation has come to an end (or even if you just want to indicate that you'd like it to come to an end!), you can say something like *Jaha, ska vi äta nu?* ('Right, shall we eat now?'), or a simple *jaha* on its own.

Either way, it's a useful word to add to your Swedish vocabulary for plenty of occasions when you're not quite sure what else to say.

Jaha, nu förstår jag.
Ah/Aha, now I understand.

Jaha, ska vi gå ut nu?
Right then, shall we go out now?

Jajamänsan **'Yes indeedy'** INTERJECTION

jaj:amɛn:san

Jajamänsan looks slightly ridiculous written down. In fact, you will often see it spelled *jajamensan*, but the official Swedish dictionary uses *ä*.

Basically, it's a very long, often exaggerated or ironic, way of saying 'yes' (*ja*).

Answering questions with *ja ja* or even *ja ja ja* is not uncommon in Swedish, meaning 'yes yes yes!' or 'yes, absolutely'. To make your 'yes yes' even more emphatic, you can extend it to *jajamän* or *jajamänsan*.

The phrase *jajamän* has existed for a long time in Swedish, and it was a way of quickly saying *ja, heliga män* ('yes, holy men' or 'yes, by God').

The *-san* is a shortening of *sade han* ('said he'). In spoken Swedish, you often drop the last syllable of verbs like *sade*, and *-san* appears in a few other Swedish interjections including *hoppsan* ('oops') and *hejsan* ('hello').

So, *jajamänsan* is a way of agreeing strongly and emphatically, like *ja, precis* ('yes, exactly') or *absolut* ('absolutely'), but more fun to say.

A word of caution. *Jajamänsan* is very colloquial and informal Swedish, but it's not the most modern or cool language — you're more likely to hear a middle-aged parent say it than their teenage children, or in other contexts where people are acting unnaturally enthusiastic, such as game show contestants on TV. An English equivalent might be 'yes, indeedy!'

And for those of you wondering if there's an equivalent for the word 'no'? *Jajamänsan*, there is, and it's *nänämänsan* (from *nej män*).

Vi var inte säkra, men sen googlade vi och jajamänsan, det stämmer.
We weren't sure but then we googled it and yes indeed, it's right.

Är du redo? Jajamänsan!
Are you ready? I sure am!

Jo 'Yes' (in response to a negated question or statement) INTERJECTION

ju:

Jo and *ja* both mean 'yes' in Swedish. But when do you use one or the other?

A reasonably simple rule to remember is that *ja* is used for affirmative answers to positive questions...

-Talar du svenska? -Ja ('Do you speak Swedish? -Yes')

... and *jo* is used when answering negated questions in the affirmative:

-Talar du inte svenska? -Jo ('Don't you speak Swedish? -Yes [I do]')

Jo is also often used as a more insistent yes:

- I don't want *fika. Jooo*, just a cinnamon bun!

Or when arguing with someone: *-Nej! -Jo! -Nej! -Jo!*

In other words, it is used to mark that the answer to a negative question is not what might have been expected or to express an opinion which is different from what someone else just said. But it can also express reluctant agreement (*jo, men...* 'yes, but...') or be used at the start of a sentence to make sure you have people's attention before you get to the point, the same way an English speaker might use 'well'.

Jo may be a short interjection, but it is full of nuances that can be interpreted differently depending on tone of voice, inflection or use of extra words: the more insistent *joho*, *jojomen*, *jodå*, *jo visst*, or the slightly less certain *jovars*. And an impressed *jo jo* can be used to mean 'well, well'.

To confuse matters further, in northern Sweden the word *jo* is used more frequently and in a wider range of contexts, and is often interchangeable with *ja*. It is often also inhaled, creating a strange sound that sounds more like a gasp than a word.

- Kommer du inte?
- Jo, jag ska bara göra en grej först.
- Aren't you coming?
- Yes, I'm just going to do a thing first.

- Svenska är inte ett svårt språk.
- Jo, det är det!
- Swedish is not a difficult language.
- Yes, it is!

Jul **'Christmas'** NOUN

ju:l

You'll hear this word in December as part of the greeting *God Jul!* ('Merry Christmas!') and as a prefix that makes just about any word more festive, such as *julsång* ('Christmas song'), *julstämning* ('Christmas atmosphere'), *julhandla* ('to shop for Christmas gifts and items'), *julmat* ('Christmas food'), *julstäda* ('to clean the house for Christmas')... we could go on.

And on and on. If there's one thing Swedes enjoy more than holiday preparations, it's creating compound words. Another option is to turn *jul* into an adjective: *julig* means 'Christmassy'.

English speakers might spy a resemblance to the outdated term 'yule', and there are related words in most Nordic languages: Norwegian and Danish *jul*, Icelandic *jól*, and Finnish *joulua*. All these words share an origin in Old Norse *jól* and can be traced further back to similar words in proto-Germanic languages.

In both English and Swedish today, *jul*/'yule' is a specific reference to Christmas: the Christian holiday and the surrounding season.

But that wasn't always so.

The meaning of older forms of the word *jul* were used to define different parts of the winter season depending on where in Sweden or Scandinavia the speaker was located.

In fact, language historians aren't sure exactly where it originally came from or what it meant in the earliest times, whether it was always linked to a specific festival or feast, or started out as a more general term for the winter season. The only thing that's known for certain is that it predates the celebration of Christian Christmas, and that you'll hear it a lot throughout December in Sweden.

Hur firar du jul i år?
What are you doing for Christmas this year?

Snart är det jul!
It's nearly Christmas!

Julgransplundring 'Plundering of the Christmas tree'

NOUN

jʉ:lgransplɵn:drɪŋ

The word *julgransplundring* introduces you to one of Sweden's surprising winter traditions.

January 13th is officially the 20th and final day of Swedish Christmas. Yes, 20th.

It's traditionally celebrated with the *julgransplundring* or 'Christmas tree plundering', which marks the end of the festive season, when the tree is stripped of its ornaments and disposed of. Alternative names are *julgransskakning* (literally 'Christmas tree shaking') or *Knutsfest* ('St. Knut's Day').

The celebrations, which have remained mostly the same since the late 1800s, typically start with a last dance around the tree, perhaps with a song, before removing the decorations.

That means that if you've had the willpower to make them last this long, it's finally time to eat the chocolate decorations and candy canes from the tree, and to smash and eat any gingerbread houses.

There are usually a few games and songs, and especially the 1901 favourite *Raska fötter springa tripp, tripp, tripp* ('quick footsteps running, tap tap tap') which takes you through the Swedish holiday season, from the wrapping of *julklappar* to the *julgransplundring*.

Then, the tree is taken away, along with all the Christmas

decorations. If you leave an Advent star (another classic Swedish decoration, hung in the window) up until the end of January, you can expect disapproving looks from the neighbours.

In centuries gone by, Swedes would toss the tree straight out of the window onto the street, but it's important to note that this messy and not so environmentally-friendly technique isn't the done thing any more. Instead, you should take them to the designated area in your local authority. If in doubt, check with your landlord or the head of your tenant-owners' association (*bostadsrättsförening*).

Julgransplundring är en gammal tradition i Sverige.
The plundering of the Christmas tree is an old tradition in Sweden.

Dags för julgransplundring!
Time to plunder the Christmas tree!

Julklapp **'Christmas present'** NOUN

jʉːlklapː

At first glance, this word might be confusing, since the usual Swedish translation for the noun 'present' is simply *en present*.

Normally in Swedish, *en klapp* means 'a clap' or 'a tap/pat'. One context you'll often hear it in is the phrase *en klapp på axeln* ('a pat on the shoulder') which is used in the same sense as the English idiom. So what's it got to do with Christmas presents?

If you were to travel back in time and experience Swedish Christmas several centuries ago, you wouldn't find the locals shopping for chocolates or toys. Instead, Sweden had a tradition of gift-giving almost reminiscent of American Halloween trick-or-treating.

Swedes would knock on the doors of friends and neighbours before leaving behind a small token gift anonymously, perhaps a straw or wooden ornament, usually made by hand. Often these were accompanied by a small gift tag with a jokey riddle or poem that explained the meaning of the present.

So the word *julklapp* referred to *en klapp på dörren* ('a knock on the door'), the tell-tale sign that the gift had arrived. The noun was first recorded in the Swedish language in 1741. Before this time, it was generally only the upper classes who gave out holiday gifts, and those were usually exchanged at the New Year rather than on Christmas.

It wasn't until the later 19th and 20th century that it became more common to buy Christmas gifts, rather than make small items, as Sweden underwent industrialisation and incomes rose. But though the traditions may have changed, the word *julklapp* has survived in the Swedish language and remains a key part of the festive vocabulary to this day.

According to different traditions, in Sweden the presents might be given by the *jultomte* (a Swedish alternative to Santa Claus). Centuries ago, though, this task was given to, er, the Christmas goat, possibly due to a link with the Norse God Thor, who rode a chariot pulled by goats. In other families, the presents are simply left under the Christmas tree or exchanged between family members on Christmas Eve.

If you want to say you received something 'as a Christmas present', you use the preposition *i*, for example: *Jag har fått ett par vantar i julklapp av min pappa* ('I got a pair of mittens as a Christmas present from my dad').

Jultomten har delat ut julklapparna.
Santa handed out the Christmas presents.

Jag fick den i julklapp.
I got it as a Christmas present.

Kanelbulle **'Cinnamon bun'** NOUN

kane:lbəl:ɛ

The *kanelbulle* is the tastiest symbol of Sweden there is, and is celebrated every year on October 4th: *kanelbullens dag* or 'Cinnamon Bun Day'.

In the 1920s, cinnamon buns rose to their sugary fame following wartime rationing and have been deeply connected to the Swedish culture ever since. Today, they are Sweden's most beloved pastry and exist in all shapes and sizes — from the traditional ones to some with colourful toppings or filled with blueberries.

The tradition of *kanelbullens dag* ('Cinnamon Bun Day') was invented in 1999 when Sweden's Home Baking Council tried to think of ways to celebrate the organisation's 40th anniversary. Perfectly gauging the tastes of a nation, it announced the introduction of an annual feast day that has grown in popularity ever since, with around seven million cinnamon buns bought on this day alone each year.

The word *kanelbulle* is sometimes used to describe the @ symbol, which is also called *snabel-a* ('elephant's trunk a'), because of the way it looks.

While *kanelbullar* are the de facto national pastry in Sweden, of course variants exist elsewhere; the Danish version is known as 'cinnamon snail'.

But watch out: in Finnish, the pastries are called *örfil* — which means something very different in Sweden, namely a 'slap' or 'hit'. So Finnish speakers should be careful with their bakery order if they want to avoid a slap in the face.

Jag vill ha en kanelbulle, tack.
I would like a cinnamon bun, please.

Va?! Tycker du inte om kanelbullar?
What?! Don't you like cinnamon buns?

Hennes ord kom som en örfil.
Her words were like a slap in the face.

Count yourself lucky it's not Danish

The Nordic languages are Swedish, Norwegian, Danish, Icelandic and Finnish. Although Finnish stands out as different from the other ones, each language has its own quirks. This is how you count to ten in Swedish, Norwegian, Danish, Icelandic and Finnish.

	Swedish	Norwegian	Danish	Icelandic	Finnish
1	*ett*	*en*	*en*	*einn*	*yksi*
2	*två*	*to*	*to*	*tveir*	*kaksi*
3	*tre*	*tre*	*tre*	*þrír*	*kolme*
4	*fyra*	*fire*	*fire*	*fjórir*	*neljä*
5	*fem*	*fem*	*fem*	*fimm*	*viisi*
6	*sex*	*seks*	*seks*	*sex*	*kuusi*
7	*sju*	*sju/syv*	*syv*	*sjö*	*seitsemän*
8	*åtta*	*åtte*	*otte*	*átta*	*kahdeksan*
9	*nio*	*ni*	*ni*	*níu*	*yhdeksän*
10	*tio*	*ti*	*ti*	*tíu*	*kymmenen*

Swedish learners are lucky as Swedish numbers follow the same decimal system as English. But in neighbouring country Denmark, counting is another story, as Danish doesn't use a decimal system (based on the number 10) but a vigesimal system (based on the number 20). On top of that, they present the numbers in a different order. For example:

20	***tyve***	twenty
21	***enogtyve***	'one and twenty'
22	***toogtyve***	'two and twenty'
23	***treogtyve***	'three and twenty'
	…	
30	***tredive***	thirty
40	***fyrre***	forty
50	**halvtreds**	'halfway to threes'*
60	**tres**	'threes'*
70	**halvfjerds**	'halfway to fours'*
80	**firs**	'fours'*
90	**halvfems**	'halfway to fives'*

Can you figure out what the following Danish numbers are?

treoghalvtreds ***otteogtres*** ***fireoghalvfjerds***
syvoghalvtreds ***otteoghalvfems*** ***femogfirs***

treoghalvtreds = 53 ◊ otteogtres = 68 ◊ fireoghalvfjerds = 74 ◊ syvoghalvtreds = 57 ◊ otteoghalvfems = 98 ◊ femogfirs = 85

* times 20(!)

Kille 'Guy' NOUN

kɪl:ɛ

The word *kille* can refer to a young (or wannabe young) man or to someone's boyfriend.

There's no hard and fast rule dictating when a boy stops being a *pojke* and becomes a *kille*, or when a *kille* becomes a *man*, so there are overlaps in terms of age. Generally, you can use *kille* from the teenage years and to describe men in their 20s and 30s.

Context plays a part too: *kille* started out as a slang word and is a more informal term than *man*, similar to 'guy' in English, or 'bloke' in British English. But it is becoming more and more commonly used, and unlike 'guy' or 'bloke' you'll see it in some formal contexts, like news articles. This is probably because newspapers like brevity, and using *kille* instead of man gets more information about the person's age across without using extra words.

When used with a possessive pronoun, it usually means 'boyfriend', so a person referring to *min kille* is talking about their partner. Note the difference between *Jag ska träffa en kille i kväll* ('I'm meeting a guy for a date tonight') and *Jag ska träffa min kille i kväll* ('I'm meeting my boyfriend tonight'). In the first example, there's no existing relationship between the two.

Some related words are: *killkväll* ('guys' night'), *killkläder* ('men's clothes', almost always targeting the younger demographic), and *killkompis* ('guy friend'), for example.

As for where this word comes from, it's linked to the English word 'kid', which has been used both as the name for young goats and an informal term for young children for several centuries. Both English 'kid' and the Swedish equivalent come from the Old Norse word *kið*, which meant 'young goat'.

Jag och min kille har varit tillsammans i tre år.
My boyfriend and I have been together for three years.

En kille blev rånad på tisdagskvällen.
A young man was robbed on Tuesday evening.

Kollektivavtal 'Collective bargaining agreement'

NOUN

kɔlɛkti:vavtɑ:l

This Swedish word is very useful to know if you're job-searching or experiencing problems at work.

Kollektivavtal can be broken down into two words: *kollektiv* ('collective') and *avtal* ('deal'). The English language translation would be 'collective bargaining agreement', and it refers to a set of working conditions agreed between employers and union representatives.

You'll hear this word a lot in Sweden, where around 90 percent of employees are covered by a *kollektivavtal.*

A *kollektivavtal* will regulate wages, for example stipulating that all employees with a certain job title must receive a salary within a set pay band, as well as holiday allowance, overtime pay, working hours, and other benefits.

The agreement applies to all employees at the company, even those who are not members of the union. It's possible to have clauses that only cover a certain category of employees, though. For example, it's relatively common for a *kollektivavtal* to include an extra week of holiday for workers aged over 40.

The big advantage of a *kollektivavtal* is that they offer employees more favourable conditions than workplaces without these agreements. For example, the Annual Leave Act dictates that employees must receive no fewer than 25 days of holiday, and a *kollektivavtal* can offer more than this, but not less.

The opposing argument is that the *kollektivavtal* limits the ability of individual employees to negotiate. For example, if you've had a particularly successful year at work, you might go into your annual review hoping to argue the case for a significant pay rise, but if your workplace is governed by a *kollektivavtal*, this might just not be possible.

> ***Har ni kollektivavtal?***
> Do you have a collective bargaining agreement?*

> ***Ett kollektivavtal är faktiskt flera avtal som gäller lön, semester, pension, med mera.***
> A collective bargaining agreement is actually several agreements which apply to wages, holidays, pension and more.

* An important question to ask at job interviews.

Kosläpp **'Release of the cows'** NOUN

ku:slɛp:

Kosläpp is used to describe the day when Swedish farmers release their cows.

Specifically, it's when cows are let back out into the fields after a winter spent indoors, since Swedish animal welfare laws require that cows be allowed to graze outside during the summer.

The cows are excited to be out in the open after the long winter — a feeling anyone living in Sweden can relate to — and their first reaction to being let out of the barns is usually to run and jump around the pasture, roll around in the grass, and generally frolic in the fresh air.

The Swedish idiom *glad/yster som en kalv på grönbete* ('happy/frisky as a calf on pasture') sums up the cows' reaction.

These days it's become popular for Swedes to attend a *kosläpp* at local farms, often with their families, ever since dairy cooperative Arla started selling tickets to the *kosläpp* some years ago. Farms will usually organise other activities too, such as games for children or talks about the animals and machinery, and light refreshments may be served. These days, it's even possible to attend the events online by watching livestreams of the big moment, which shows how important the date has become.

Kosläpp is a newer name for the event, which is 'officially' known as *betessläpp*. Both words come from the phrase *släppa ut* ('to release/let out'), and *bete* ('pasture') while *ko* means 'cow'. Like the English word 'cow', *ko* is used to refer to cattle whether male or female, but can also be used to describe female cows as well as females of some other species, for example *älgko* is used to refer to an adult female elk.

To say the phrase 'go to/attend the *kosläpp*', you use the preposition *på*: *Jag vill gå på kosläppet* ('I want to go to the release of the cows').

Snart är det dags för årets kosläpp.
It's nearly time for this year's cow-release.

Ska vi gå på kosläppet i morgon?
Shall we go to the release of the cows tomorrow?

Krog 'Pub'; 'restaurant'; 'canteen'; 'bar'; 'nightclub'

NOUN

kɾuːg

A *krog* is a Swedish pub.

Like many European languages, Swedish makes a distinction between restaurants (*restaurang* in Swedish), where the focus is on the food, and pubs, where you go primarily to drink.

A traditional *krog* would offer only classic *husmanskost* or hearty, simple fare such as meatballs and mashed potatoes, and you could spend the evening there without needing to order food.

But these days, the distinction between *krog* and *restaurang* isn't so clear. Many eateries with the name *krog* might serve quite elegant food (you could refer to them as a *lyxkrog* or 'luxurious pub'), and you'll also find *krogar* serving food of many different cuisines: you might hear about an *indisk krog* ('Indian pub') or *fransk krog* ('French pub'), for example.

The word *krog* evokes a specific, traditional kind of socialising, as you can tell from words like *krogrunda* (roughly 'pub crawl', an evening spent visiting multiple pubs), *krogliv* ('pub-focused nightlife'), *krogmiljö* ('pub environment') and at the less positive end of the spectrum, *krogbråk* (an argument or scuffle that breaks out at a pub).

And if you ever find yourself on a road trip around Sweden, you should look out for a *vägkrog*, literally meaning 'road pub'.

These are more like canteens or fast food restaurants than classic pubs, located close to a busy road, where you can often stop and get a warming bite to eat before going on your way.

Det finns en mysig krog i stan.
There's a cosy pub downtown.

Vi kan stanna och äta lunch på någon vägkrog.
We can stop for lunch at some roadside pub along the way.

Leg **'Proof of ID'** NOUN

lɛg:

If you're out drinking with a Swede and they return from the bar telling you, often with thinly veiled pride, that they had to show the bartender their *leg* to buy a pint: fear not, it's not that kind of pub.

Leg is short for *legitimation* or your identification document.

It comes from the Medieval Latin *legitimationem*, from the verb *legitimare* which means 'make lawful' or 'declare to be lawful'.

In Swedish, the short form *leg* (alternative spelling: *legg*) is becoming increasingly common, but the longer *legitimation* is still used sometimes. Perhaps slightly confusingly, the two words take different genders: it's *ett leg* but *en legitimation*.

The word *legitimation* is also used to explain that someone is allowed to carry out certain professional duties, for example like a certified or licensed doctor (*legitimerad läkare* or *läkarlegitimation*).

The Swedish word for 'leg' by the way (as in the limbs connected to your feet), is *ben*, which also means 'bone'.

Personnummer och legitimation, tack.
Social security number and ID, please.

Lillördag 'Little Saturday' NOUN

lɪl:œ:ɖa

Lillördag means 'little Saturday', from *lilla* ('little') and *lördag* ('Saturday'). Today, it's an alternative word for… 'Wednesday'.

But why?

In times gone by, maids and servants often had to work on Saturdays, and were given one weekday off work instead, usually midweek. So Wednesday (*onsdag* in Swedish, getting its name from Nordic god Odin) was given the nickname *piglördag*, from the word *piga* which means 'maid' or 'servant': 'servant Saturday'.

Piglördag was also called *lillördag*, and as it became less and less common to have household staff, *lillördag* was used more and more.

Over time, the meaning changed too.

Lillördag has now become an excuse for midweek drinks and activities, so you might go for an *afterwork* to celebrate. Some bars and restaurants open late or even have special offers.

An appropriate English translation for *lillördag* might be 'hump day'. So feel free to use the phrase *Det är ju lillördag!* ('It's hump day, after all!') to justify any midweek treat, or to add *#lillördag* to your Instagram posts while out celebrating on Wednesday night.

Lördag itself has an interesting history.

The Swedish name for Saturday comes from the Old Norse name *laugardagr* which meant 'bathing day'. *Laug* meant 'pool' or 'lake' and *dagr* meant 'day'.

Vikings are believed to have washed themselves once a week, on a Saturday, washing and combing their hair and beards as well. This was much more than many other people at the time, and the Vikings' personal grooming habits were commented on in many writings by foreign monks and scribes. Today, the word for Saturday in all the Scandinavian languages comes from the Old Norse word meaning 'bathing/washing day'.

Jag ska bara dricka öl på helgen... fast onsdag är ju lillördag.
I'm only going to drink beer at the weekends... but Wednesday is of course Little Saturday.

Fira lillördag hos oss!
Celebrate Little Saturday with us!*

* A slogan you might see at bars and events trying to entice in customers for midweek drinks.

Loppis **'Flea market'** NOUN

lɔpːɪs

Loppisar are a hugely popular way to spend sunny weekends as people set up makeshift stalls to buy and sell secondhand items or crafts at bargain prices.

It's common for an apartment block or entire neighbourhood to get together and organise a *loppis*, or you can head to many town squares or streets to go *loppis*-hunting.

It's not hard to see why Swedes love them so much. *Loppisar* usually take place outdoors and so allow visitors to make the most of the summer; the focus on re-using is eco-friendly; the low prices are always a bonus in expensive Sweden; and then there's the chance of finding a great vintage accessory or piece of furniture.

The full term is *loppmarknad*, or *lopptorg* in Swedish-speaking Finland, but it's common in colloquial Swedish to shorten words by knocking off the final syllable or two and adding the suffix *-is*, hence *loppis*.

To say 'at a flea market', you use the preposition *på*, for example *Ska vi gå på loppis?* ('Shall we go to a flea market?').

The longer word *loppmarknad* comes from a direct translation of the US English term 'flea market', since *en loppa* is 'a flea'. This is a nod to the fact that the markets sell secondhand clothes and furniture. Some people looked down on these and claimed they were full of fleas.

You can use the word *loppisfynd* ('flea market find' or 'flea market bargain') to refer to the treasures you track down at a *loppis*, and a *bakluckeloppis* (literally a 'car boot flea market') is a car boot sale, where instead of tables, items are sold straight out of people's cars.

While *en loppa* means flea, *ett lopp* is 'a track' or 'a run', so don't get confused between words like *maratonlopp* ('a marathon race') or major Swedish races like *Vasaloppet* (a cross-country skiing race) and *Lidingöloppet* (a well-known running race in Stockholm).

Jag har köpt den på loppis.
I bought it at a flea market.

Jag vill sälja mina gamla kläder på loppis.
I want to sell my old clothes at a flea market.

Lov 'Break' (from school or university) NOUN

lo:v

Lov is related to the English noun 'leave', and the link to holiday or vacation is clear if you think about 'leaving a place' or the noun in 'a leave of absence'. In Swedish, *lov* has two main other meanings: 'praise' and 'permission'.

It has been used to mean 'permission to be absent from school' or 'school break' for at least 400 years. You can't use *lov* when you talk about being away from work, though. In that case, the word for 'holiday' or 'vacation' is *semester*.

Sweden's main school holidays are *sommarlov* ('summer break'), *påsklov* ('Easter break'), *jullov* ('Christmas break'), *sportlov* ('sports break', used to refer to the late winter holiday when people typically travel to winter sports resorts) and *höstlov* ('autumn break') which has been re-named *läslov* ('reading break') to encourage children to read.

While today these are recreational times, that wasn't always the case.

Sommarlov was first introduced back in the 19th century, with the aim that youngsters spend the break helping their parents with work. At this time, Sweden was an agricultural economy and summer was the busiest time on farms. These days children are less likely to spend the break working, and Swedish schoolchildren benefit from one of the world's longest summer breaks, at around ten weeks in total.

Sportlov was introduced during the Second World War after a recommendation by the government-run energy commission that Sweden could save fuel by not having to heat up the country's schools for a week during one of the coldest months of the year.

Sportlov was initially named *kokslov* (named after coke, the high-carbon content fuel), but eventually changed its name to match the winter sports activities on offer for the children on vacation. In the 1950s, public health services noted that this was the peak season for Swedish children catching the flu or norovirus, and by keeping them away from the schools for a week, the spreading of such illnesses reduced drastically. The Swedish government then decided to retain the vacation.

Vi ska åka till Småland på lovet.
We will go to Småland during the break.

Sommarlovet är äntligen här!
The summer break is here at last!

Lugn **'Calm'** ADJECTIVE

lɵŋːn

Lugn means 'calm', 'tranquil', 'serene' or 'relaxed'. You can use it to describe a permanent state or a temporary condition. So if you say *Det är en lugn gata* ('It's a calm/quiet street'), it means that it is a street where there's never much noise or traffic, but if you say *Det var lugnt på gatan* ('The street was quiet'), that just refers to a particular point in time.

When you describe a person, the tense changes the meaning of *lugn* even more.

If you say *Han var lugn* ('He was calm'), this can mean 'calm', 'unperturbed', 'unworried', 'unbothered' or 'relaxed', and you'd usually be describing the person's state in reaction to a specific incident.

But if you say something like *Han är en lugn person* ('He is a calm person'), it's a reference to temperament, implying that nothing ever really bothers him, or describing someone who is cool-headed and rational.

Lugn also refers to calm, soothing sounds, for example in the name of the Stockholm radio station *Lugna klassiker* which you'll often hear in taxis or at airports, playing chilled-out tunes.

Lugn can be used as a noun (*ett lugn*) meaning 'the tranquility/calmness'. For example: *Till slut kom lugnet* ('In the end, all was calm'). And it can be transformed into an adverb, *lugnt*, which you'll often hear in the phrase *Ta det lugnt!* ('Take it easy!').

In Old Swedish, *lugn* (or *lygn* as it was sometimes spelled) referred specifically to the calm, still surface of a lake. It shares an etymology with the word 'lagoon', a shallow body of water which usually has a calm surface due to its depth and isolation.

Lugn has a verb form, *lugna* ('to calm, to quieten'), which most often appears in the phrase *lugna ner* ('to calm/quieten down'). For example: *Du måste lugna ner hunden!* ('You need to calm the dog down!'); *När han lugnat ner sig ska han kunna somna* ('When he calms down he'll be able to sleep').

Tekniker som meditation kan ge lugn även i en stressig miljö.
Techniques like meditation can bring calm even to stressful environments.

Jag får aldrig en lugn stund!
I never get a moment of peace!

Lördagsgodis 'Pick'n'mix sweets on a Saturday' NOUN

lœːɖasguːdɪs

This word means 'Saturday sweets' or 'Saturday candy'. *Lördag* is the Swedish name for 'Saturday' (see *lillördag* to learn more about where it comes from). *Godis* meanwhile means 'sweets' or 'candy', and is a shortening of the term *godsaker* (literally 'good/tasty things'). *Godis* is a countable noun, like British English 'sweet' but unlike American English 'candy', so you can have *en godis* ('one sweet/one piece of candy') or *två/tio/hundratals godisar* ('two/ten/hundreds of sweets or pieces of candy').

Lördagsgodis refers to the Swedish tradition of stocking up on sweets at the weekend, usually from the pick'n'mix aisle in the supermarket, or the *godisvägg* ('wall of candy') as it's sometimes called.

Pick'n'mix is called *plockgodis* ('candy for plucking') in Swedish, *smågodis* ('small sweets') or *lösgodis* ('loose sweets'). These days, there's often an option to fill up on *naturgodis* instead (literally 'natural candy', referring to nuts, seeds, berries and dried fruit, also served pick'n'mix style).

Each Saturday you'll see many families with small children (and adults too!) filling up their paper bags with the sweet stuff.

But this tradition has a very murky past.

In the late 1950s, a series of experiments were carried out on patients in mental health hospitals, and these unethical tests were the origin of *lördagsgodis*.

During the Vipeholm Experiments, named after the hospital in Lund where they took place, patients were encouraged to eat huge amounts of sugary sweets in a deliberate attempt to get cavities in their teeth, so that scientists could research the link between sugar and dental health, which was unclear at the time, and how to treat them. Different groups were given sweets to eat either daily or once a week.

The researchers discovered that there was indeed a clear link between high sugar consumption and teeth cavities, but also that the groups eating lots of sweets only once a week got fewer cavities than those who ate a little each day. And so the Medicines Agency recommended that Swedes limit their candy-eating to once a week rather than small daily snacks — although pick'n'mix-style loose candy wasn't allowed in Sweden until 1985. Before that, you had to stock up on your salty liquorice and fudge (two of the most popular sweets in Sweden) at an old-fashioned sweet shop.

Lördagsgodis är alltid en bra idé!
Having sweets on Saturday is always a good idea!

Lördagsgodis är ett unikt svenskt fenomen.
Having sweets on Saturday is a uniquely Swedish phenomenon.

Matte & husse 'Pet owner' NOUN

mat:ɛ hɵs:ɛ

Matte is a shortening of *matmor* (literally 'food mother') which can mean either 'housewife', 'homemaker' or 'pet owner'. The male equivalent is *husse*, which comes from the word *husbonde*, related to English 'husband'. It literally meant something like 'dweller of the house' (*bonde* comes from the verb *bo*, 'to reside') and was used to mean 'head of the household'.

These days the words *matmor* and *husbonde* are just as old-fashioned as the traditional gender roles they describe, so you are unlikely to hear them in Swedish. But you will hear pet owners refer to themselves as *matte* and *husse*.

There are other synonyms you could use instead if you prefer. In a formal setting, you should stick to saying something like *Jag har husdjur* ('I have pets') or *Jag är hundägare* ('I am a dog owner') instead.

For more colloquial contexts, a word of caution about directly translating the English terms 'dog mum/cat mum'. *Hundmamma* and *kattmamma* in Swedish generally refer to the animal themselves, in other words to a dog or a cat with babies.

But you will hear Swedish pet owners, especially younger ones, calling themselves *mamma* or *pappa* ('mum' or 'dad') instead of *husse* or *matte* when talking to their animal, for example *Mamma/pappa älskar dig!* ('Mum/dad loves you!') instead of *Matte/husse älskar dig!* ('Your owner loves you!').

Jag vill vara en rolig matte.
I want to be a fun pet mum/pet owner.

Hunden gick fram till sin husse och slickade honom på handen.
The dog went up to his/her owner and licked his hand.

Medelsvensson **'An average person in Sweden'** NOUN

me:dɛlsfɛn:sɔn

This is a useful Swedish word to know if you're looking at statistics or talking about Swedes and Swedishness.

The word *medelsvensson* can be translated as 'typical Swede', and it's used to talk about the average Swedish inhabitant.

It comes up a lot when talking about data and statistics. For example, you might say something like *Medelsvensson dricker fem koppar kaffe varje dag* ('The typical Swede drinks five cups of coffee every day'), or a researcher might ask *Hur stor är skillnaden mellan vad en medelsvensson och de rikaste tjänar?* ('How big is the difference between what the average person and the richest earn?').

You can also use it to mean 'an ordinary person' or 'the man on the street' in other contexts.

Medel means 'average' (or 'mean' to be specific), and the term comes from the fact that Svensson is such a common name in Sweden.

As of December 2020, there were 90,221 people in Sweden with Svensson as their surname. That's counting spelling variations such as Svenson and Swenson, and the 61 men and five women who had Svensson as a first name.

In other words, nearly one in every 100 Swedes has the surname Svensson, but surprisingly that still doesn't make it the country's most common last name. In fact, it only comes ninth on the list with Andersson the most popular: 224,669 people in Sweden have the name. The next most common surnames in 2020 were Johansson, Karlsson, Nilsson, Eriksson, Larsson, Olsson, and Persson.

But the reason we talk about *medelsvensson* is that the term was first coined back in 1930, when Svensson was the most common surname in the country.

You might also hear people use the term *svenssonliv* (a 'Svensson life'), which basically means 'an average life'.

You could draw a lot of conclusions from the popularity of these terms, and many people would point to Sweden's reputation as a culture which prizes conformity and egalitarianism. As the country develops, partly due to globalisation and partly due to immigration, it remains to be seen how the concept of the *medelsvensson* will change.

Medelsvensson heter faktiskt Andersson i efternamn.
The typical Swede actually has the surname Andersson.

Familjen Medelsvensson har förändrats under årens lopp.
The typical Swedish family has changed over the years.

Earth man meets lucky cheese

What kind of people do these expressions describe?

1. ***Medelsvensson*** **'average Svensson'**
   a) someone who is always in the middle
   b) a typical Swede
   c) a descendant of the Swedish King Sven
2. ***Panelhöna*** **'panel hen'**
   a) someone who doesn't get to dance
   b) someone who is always talking
   c) interior decorator
3. ***Stugsittare*** **'cabin sitter'**
   a) house sitter
   b) someone who rarely goes out
   c) someone who is waiting for something to happen
4. ***Skitstövel*** **'shit boot'**
   a) someone who has walked really far in bad weather
   b) someone who buys many low-quality shoes
   c) someone who doesn't treat others well
5. ***Jordgubbe*** **'earth man'**
   a) strawberry
   b) farmer
   c) vegan
6. ***Lattepappa*** **'caffe latte dad'**
   a) barista
   b) father of a young child enjoying his parental leave
   c) dad trying to make friends with his teenage children by adopting new trends

7. ***Fartdåre* 'speed fool'**
   a) someone who takes hasty decisions
   b) someone who drives too fast
   c) drug addict
8. ***Hösäck* 'hay sack'**
   a) vegetarian
   b) lazy person
   c) someone with a bad posture
9. ***Lyckans ost* 'lucky cheese'**
   a) lottery winner
   b) someone who is really lucky
   c) cheesemonger
10. ***Nakenfis* 'naked fart'**
   a) naked child
   b) someone who farts openly
   c) smelly nudist
11. ***Sötnos* 'sweet nose'**
   a) cute person
   b) someone with a great sense of smell
   c) someone with a cute nose
12. ***Ynkrygg* 'pity back'**
   a) someone who feels sorry for themselves
   b) someone who is always in pain
   c) a coward

1b, 2a, 3b, 4c, 5a, 6b, 7b, 8c, 9b, 10a, 11a, 12c

Mellandagar 'Days in-between Christmas and New Year' NOUN

mɛlːandɑːgar

You know those odd few days between Christmas and New Year when time seems to lose all meaning and your diet consists mainly of Christmas leftovers and chocolate? In Swedish, there's a word for that.

Mellandagar means 'between-days' and is used to talk about the time between December 26th and January 1st, which are both public holidays in Sweden.

Those five days in-between aren't official public holidays, although many Swedish companies will give employees a full or at least half day off on December 31st and the generous ones — or those that shut down operations entirely during the holiday period — might give all five as extra days off. In workplaces where this doesn't happen, there might be a scramble over who gets to book this coveted time off as holiday. It's definitely worth asking prospective employers their policy on *mellandagar* if you ever find yourself choosing between job offers in Sweden!

This does mean that in many businesses, normal service doesn't resume until the new year, so watch out for reduced opening times during the *mellandagar* if you have errands to run.

This is also a good time of year for bargain-hunting thanks to the *mellandagsrea* or 'between-days sales' that many shops and companies offer. Or if you'd prefer to get out of town, many hotels, spas and ski resorts offer special *mellandagar* packages so you can take a break during this period.

Vi ska ha det mysigt i mellandagarna.
We're going to have a cosy, relaxing time between Christmas and New Year.

Vi har begränsade öppettider över julen och mellandagarna.
We have limited opening hours from Christmas until New Year.

Munsbit **'A small bite to eat'** NOUN

mɵn:spiːt

En munsbit is how you might describe a small slice of cake, a handful of nuts, or a canapé.

In English, you could translate it as 'a bite', 'a mouthful' or the French term *amuse-bouche*. The food can be sweet or savoury, so it's an appropriate word whether you're out for *fika*, having tapas, or snacking throughout the day.

It's a compound word made up of *mun* ('mouth') and *bit*, which can mean 'piece' or 'bit'.

And *munsbit* has a metaphorical use too: a useful nugget of information could be *en munsbit*.

It can also refer to battles or conflicts in which one party easily defeats the other: the losers are described as *en munsbit* for the victors.

One of the most common metaphorical uses is in sports, so when the Swedish football team knocked Italy out of the World Cup in 2017, a lot of euphoric Swedes declared that Italy was a *munsbit* — meaning it didn't take long to finish them off. A rough English translation might be '[the winners] had them for breakfast'.

Munsbit is an old word, dating back to at least the early 18th century. But you'll hear a lot of Swedes use the word *mumsbit* (with an *m*) in its place. *Mums* means 'yum', so because it can be hard to tell the difference between *n* and *m* in speech, and because both *mums* and *munsbit* have similar meanings, a lot of people think this is the original word.

In linguistics, this is called folk etymology, a phenomenon when an old word is reinterpreted using familiar words that make logical sense (another example is *handburgare*, a word used by many young Swedes instead of the dictionary-approved *hamburgare*, because you often eat burgers using your hands). And because language is determined by use and not by dictionaries, these days it's fair to say that *mumsbit* is a word in its own right.

> ***Vilken mumsig munsbit.***
> That was a tasty snack.
>
> ***Danmark är alltid en munsbit för Sverige.***
> Denmark are always easy pickings for Sweden.*

---

* About sports teams.

Myndighet **'Public authority'** NOUN

myn:dɪhe:t

In Sweden, *myndighet* often refers specifically to the *statliga myndigheter* or 'state agencies'. But you can also talk about *regionala* or *kommunala myndigheter* ('regional' or 'municipal authorities'), or use it to talk about authorities in other countries, for example *spanska myndigheter* ('Spanish authorities') or *lokala myndigheter* ('local authorities').

There are over 200 state agencies in Sweden, including the Swedish Migration Agency (*Migrationsverket*) and the Swedish Public Health Agency (*Folkhälsomyndigheten*) to give two examples.

This group also covers many universities and higher education institutions as well as the Swedish Police (*Polismyndigheten*), and Sweden's National Museum (*Nationalmuseum*).

As you can see, not all *myndigheter* have the word *myndighet* in their name. Several have *-verket* ('agency') or *-ombudsman* in the name instead, or something completely different.

It is written into the national constitution that Sweden's public agencies are independent of the government, although the government provides funding and usually appoints their directors. These are not political positions and people often stay in their roles even after changes of government.

Sweden's government ministries oversee different agencies

— for example the work of the Migration Agency falls under the remit of the Migration Minister — but there is generally a hands-off approach. Ministers and governments tend not to overrule agencies or disregard their advice, even when they have the power to do so.

There are two main goals of this separation: ensuring that decisions are made based on knowledge and expertise, and limiting corruption.

But a frequent criticism is that the separation leads to unnecessary red tape, delays and a lack of accountability for problems. For example, there may be cases where the government and relevant authority both agree something is a problem, but the authority says they are simply following the law while the government defers to the agency when it comes to interpreting the law.

Det är viktigt att myndigheterna samarbetar.
It is important for the authorities to work together.

Sedan är det upp till de lokala myndigheterna.
Then it's up to the local authorities.

Mörk **'Dark'** ADJECTIVE

mœrːk

You can use *mörk* to describe a noun, for example *ett mörkt rum* ('a dark room') or *en mörk natt* ('a dark night').

It can modify a colour adjective (such as *blå* or *grön*), in which case you combine both words, like *mörkblå* ('dark blue') or *mörkgrön* ('dark green'). It can also be combined with other kinds of adjectives and adverbs, for example *mörkhårig* ('brunette', or literally 'dark-haired').

Like in English, *mörk* can be used metaphorically to talk about something sinister, not completely rational or understood, for example *mörk magi* ('dark magic or black magic') or *mörk materia* ('dark matter').

And it can mean 'gloomy' or 'negative', for example *mörka tider* ('dark times') or the phrases *teckna en mörk bild* ('to paint a gloomy picture') or *kasta en mörk skugga över någonting* ('to cast a dark cloud over something').

Mörker means 'darkness', which again can be both literal or figurative, and *mörkrädd* is 'scared of the dark'.

Like the English word 'murky' meaning 'obscured/difficult to see', *mörk* comes from the Old Norse word *myrkr* ('darkness'). In fact, up until a few hundred years ago, 'murk' existed as an adjective in English and was used by playwright William Shakespeare.

Det finns mörka krafter som väntar i kulisserna.
There are dark powers waiting behind the scenes.

Det blir mörkare ute.
It's getting darker outside.

Najs **'Lovely'** ADJECTIVE

naj:s

Here's a word that should be familiar to Swedish learners with a knowledge of English.

Najs is pronounced almost exactly the same as English 'nice', and the reason why is simple: it's a loan word, but has been adapted to fit Swedish spelling.

It can be used as a substitute for words like *trevlig*, *fin*, or *skön*, which all mean something like 'nice' in Swedish and can refer to how something looks or a general feeling, for example *Det är najs att dansa lite* ('It's nice/fun to have a bit of a dance'). But watch out, as there is often a sarcastic undertone to *najs*.

You'll also hear it as an exclamation, as in English, to express appreciation for something: *Najs!*

Over recent years, Swedish has borrowed plenty of words from English thanks to a growing level of English language proficiency and the wide availability of English books, films, songs and games.

This is in contrast to the situation a century or so ago: the Swedish Academy has existed since the 1700s, with the goal of promoting the "purity, strength, and sublimity of the Swedish language", which for a long time meant discouraging the use of foreign words.

But today, there are lots of English loan words in Swedish.

Sometimes, they'll keep their English spelling, especially if they're recent borrowings. But the more they are used, the more integrated into the Swedish language they become.

The first stage of this is usually adapting to Swedish grammar. For example, *callcenter* is usually written as one word in Swedish, which favours compound words. And commonly used verbs, like *googla* ('to Google'), *snooza* (not quite 'to snooze', but 'to press the snooze button on an alarm' or 'to temporarily delay') or *attacha* ('to attach' — an alternative to Swedish *bifoga*), usually take on the Swedish verb endings such as *-a* in the infinitive or basic form and *-ar* in the present tense: *jag googlar* ('I Google' or 'I'm Googling').

Taking on Swedish spelling is the next stage of the loan word's integration, and it's more likely to happen the more common a word is. *Najs* is quite a common word, and heavy usage probably sped up its Swedification.

As for why so many Swedes, especially young Stockholmers, prefer *najs* to the Swedish alternatives, it's probably down to a perceived cool status of the English language, or simply a desire to switch things up a bit.

Other words which have been adapted into Swedish in the same way include *dejt* ('date', but only in the romantic sense), *tejp* ('tape') and *tajt* ('tight').

And you may also be interested to learn that 'nice' itself wasn't always such a nice word. It started out as a negative term, which came from the Latin *nescius* meaning 'ignorant'.

That was the meaning when it first entered the English language in the 13th century, but over the years the meaning changed, first to 'timid', then to 'fussy/fastidious', then 'careful/precise' and eventually 'agreeable/kind'.

Parken kommer att bli riktigt najs på sommaren.
The park will be lovely in the summer.

Najs klänning!
Nice dress!

Najs keps!

In English, there are a few Swedish loanwords, such as 'smorgasbord', 'orienteering', and 'moped'. Obviously, things work the other way around and many English words have been adapted in pronunciation, spelling and meaning. As an S doesn't signal plurality in Swedish it's often kept in the singular form.

SWEDISH	INSPIRED BY	ENGLISH
mejl	**email**	email
tejp	**tape**	cellotape
tajt	**tight**	tight (clothing)
muffins	**muffins**	muffin
lajv	**live**	live action role playing game (LARP)

Can you guess what English words the following Swedish ones are inspired by and what they mean?

räls kex keps fejk

räls – rails – railway track ◊ *kex* – cakes – biscuit ◊ *keps* – caps – cap ◊ *fejk* – fake – fake

***Nja* 'Yes and no'** INTERJECTION

nja: or njɑ:

Nja is a jumble of the words *nej* ('no') and *ja* ('yes'), which you can use when you don't want to express an opinion on something outright. That might be because you don't have the information to give a concrete answer yet, or because you just don't want to pick a side. There's a similar construction in German: *jein*, from *ja* ('yes') and *nein* ('no').

So it might express hesitation or disagreement. Depending on the context, the English equivalent might be something like 'We-ell…', 'yes and no…'. It's a perfect word to pull out if you're put on the spot in a debate and need to give a non-committal response.

Nja is often used like a counterpart of *jo*. *Jo* means 'yes', when answering a question posed in the negative, for example: *Tycker du inte om djur? Jo* ('Don't you like animals? Yes, I do'). And *nja* can be used to respond negatively to questions, without giving an outright denial: *Talar du svenska? Nja…* ('Do you speak Swedish? Well, sort of, but…').

If you're trying to work out what Swedish-speaking friends really mean with their *nja*, remember it's usually slightly closer to the 'no' end of the yes-no spectrum.

To really emphasise the doubt or hesitation, you can draw out the word for longer: *njaaaa…*

Men ni är väl vänner? – Nja, inte vänner direkt.
But you're friends, right? – Well, not really 'friends'.

Alla tycker ju om kaffe – Nja, jag tycker bättre om te.
Everyone likes coffee – Well, I like tea more.

Nollåtta 'Stockholmer' NOUN

nɔlːɔtːa

You can still hear this Swedish relic from the pre-mobile phone age, sometimes even in Stockholm.

Nollåtta, from the Stockholm dialling code 08-, (*noll* is 'zero', *åtta* is 'eight'), still functions as a pejorative shorthand for a *Stockholmare* or person from Stockholm, even as landlines become rarer.

The dialling code in central Stockholm was changed to 08- back in 1963. Then in 1992, the then state telecoms company Televerket moved those in the wider Stockholm region, who had previously been 07-, onto 08- to free up a new set of numbers for the emerging mobile phones.

Nollåtta today is generally used as a mild insult or as a piece of friendly banter targeted at people hailing from the capital. The noun is often preceded by a strengthening adjective such as *jäkla* ('damned') or *förbannade* ('accursed').

Stockholmers living and working in a northern Swedish town might find their colleagues jokingly — or perhaps only half-jokingly — berating them with *Din jäkla nollåtta!* ('You bloody Stockholmer!').

If a Stockholmer living in the Swedish provinces dares to give any impression that they consider themselves more educated or skilled than the locals, they should expect to find the words *typisk nollåtta* ('typical Stockholmer') snorted behind their backs, in disdain at their perceived arrogance.

Among Stockholmers themselves, the moniker has become a source of pride.

Stockholmers living in the regions, or on a visit, might self-mockingly point out some of their big city habits, with the words: *Jag vet, typisk nollåtta* ('I know, typical Stockholmer').

On August 8th, 2008 — or in Swedish dating convention 080808 — Stockholm even held a citywide '08 day' celebration, with dance floors set up outside the City Hall and in nightclub district Stureplan with free breakfast and karaoke on offer in the Stockholm Globe Arena.

Du jäkla nollåtta.
You bloody Stockholmer.

Jag är ingen nollåtta.
I'm no Stockholmer.

Nämen 'Oh gosh' INTERJECTION

nɛmɛn:

Swedes are not a people prone to big reactions. But once in a while you may hear a mildly surprised Swede step out of their shell and exclaim ... *nämen!*

Nämen comes from the words *nej* and *men* which literally mean 'no' and 'but'.

It is used, often at the start of a sentence, to express mild surprise in a positive, neutral or negative sense: '*Nämen*, what a cute dog!' Or draw out the second syllable for effect: *Nämennnnnn* if it's a really cute dog.

It's a bit like saying 'oh' in English, or 'gosh', or 'well, well, well!'

Nämen can also stand on its own, if said with the right emphasis. If, for example, you run into a friend you haven't seen in a while, you can shout *Nämen!* when you spot them. With just one little word you can say 'Fancy seeing you here! Long time no see! I've missed you, old pal'. Swedish is a wonderfully efficient language.

It can also be used as one of those words at the start of a sentence before you get to what you actually want to say (much like 'well' in English). '*Nämen*, should we start thinking of going home?'

Nämen, hej.
Well, hello.

Nämen, vad duktig du är.
Wow, you're so good.

Ockerhyra **'Overpriced rent'** NOUN

ɔk:ɛɾhy:ɾa

The word *ocker* means 'usury' and refers to crimes like loans with unfairly high interest rates or that are otherwise unethical, especially when taking advantage of the victim in a vulnerable situation.

Hyra means rent, but *ockerhyra* isn't part of the same Swedish law. It can be used in general to refer to overpriced rentals, whether they are legal or not. But in some cases *ockerhyra* is against the law.

Sweden regulates sublets strictly; in general you aren't supposed to rent for profit and landlords should only charge a 'reasonable' rent. That means you should pay no more than the amount the landlord pays, plus an additional 10-15 percent if the apartment is furnished, and fees for any other services included in the contract.

That's fairly easy to calculate if you're subletting from someone who rents the apartment themselves, but it's harder if your landlord owns the apartment. In that case, the basic rent can be calculated based on the market value, which might be based on recently sold similar properties. Then, four percent is usually added on to cover the cost of capital.

So even if your landlord owns the property outright, they can charge you based on how much they would be paying for a brand new mortgage on it — which can be quite high in Sweden's competitive property market. Some people might refer to a highly priced sublet as *ockerhyra* even if the landlord is legally allowed to charge that amount.

If you suspect you have been a victim of *ockerhyra*, though, you can file a complaint with the Swedish Rent and Tenancy Tribunal, and may get your money back.

Många vill ha tillbaka pengar efter att ha betalat ockerhyra.
Many want their money back from overpriced renting.

Han bad om 15.000 för en tvåa, är det inte ockerhyra?
He was asking for 15,000 kronor for a two-room apartment, isn't that a rip-off?

Oj 'Oh'; 'oops' INTERJECTION

ɔjː

This little word packs quite a punch, with just two letters expressing a whole host of things: surprise, pain, shock, sympathy, embarrassment.

It's very efficient. If you bump into someone, no need for a long and wordy apology, a heartfelt *Oj!* will do and they'll understand it wasn't intentional.

If someone bumps into you, an *oj* with a slightly different tone and a frown is a way of reprimanding them — whether your *oj* is positive or negative is entirely context dependent.

In other circumstances, it might be a pleasantly surprised 'wow', a sympathetic 'oh dear', or a neutral 'oh!' or 'well!'. All of this makes it a useful word for Swedish learners to use; simply slip it into conversation whenever the occasion presents itself for a handy shortcut to fluency.

If something really surprising happens, try several in a row: *oj oj oj oj oj* — this is a sound you'll hear a lot during sports matches.

There's also the more emphatic *Ojdå!* which again can be positive or negative. And the verb *att oja sig* literally translates as 'to *oj* oneself', and can be used when someone is complaining or going on about something. *Det är inget att oja sig över* means 'It's nothing to *oj* about' or 'It's nothing to make a fuss about'.

Ojdå, något gick fel.
Oh dear, something [unclear or unexpected] went wrong.*

Oj, vad synd!
Oh, what a shame!

* A typical computer error message.

Orka 'To have the energy to do (something)' VERB

ɔr:ka

You almost always hear *orka* in the negative sense: *Jag orkar inte* means 'I don't have the energy/strength'.

You might hear non-negated sentences, such as *Du måste orka* ('You have to find the energy') or *Hjälp mig att orka!* ('Help me to cope!'), but even then there's usually an underlying sense that the activities are difficult.

Orka can refer to physical or mental energy, so *Jag orkar inte springa* ('I don't have the energy to run') could mean the speaker physically cannot run or simply that they can't be bothered. You can use it with another verb (*Jag orkar inte städa/komma/prata* — 'I don't have the energy to clean/come/talk') or on its own (*Jag orkar inte!* — 'I don't have the energy!')

Its origins date back to the Old Swedish that was used in the Middle Ages (1225-1526), when the verb was first recorded.

Another word that means the same thing is *palla*, but there's a small difference.

If someone says they don't *palla* to do something, there's a strong indication that this is their subjective opinion, not that they don't physically have the energy.

For example, if someone says *Jag ville springa efter tjuven men jag orkade inte* ('I wanted to run after the thief but I didn't have the energy'), it implies they were physically unable to, whereas the sentence *Jag pallade inte att springa efter tjuven.* ('I couldn't be bothered to run after the thief') suggests the speaker could have done it if they had wanted to.

In the past few decades, both words have evolved into an interjection (*Orka!* or *Palla!*), which is especially popular among teenagers and young people. In this context it means 'I can't be bothered!', and can be used when you don't even *orka* to string a complete sentence together.

Jag orkar inte berätta det för dig.
I can't be bothered to tell you about it.

Han pallade inte att vänta längre.
He couldn't be bothered to wait any longer.

Oväder 'Bad weather' NOUN

u:vɛ:dɛɾ

*O**väder* is a useful Swedish term without a direct one-word equivalent in English. You could translate it as 'bad weather', 'inclement weather', or 'storm', depending on the context.

On its own, the noun *väder* means 'weather', which comes from the Old Swedish term *veðr* and is related to the equivalent words in many other languages: English 'weather', German *Wetter*, Danish *vejr*, and Dutch *weer*, to name a few.

In older forms of most of these languages, including Swedish, *väder* was used specifically to refer to windy and/or rainy weather. Over time it became generalised to refer to the condition whether good or bad.

But traces of the original meaning remain in Swedish in words such as *väderkvarn* ('windmill'), and the colloquial expression *munväder* (literally 'mouth wind', meaning 'nonsense'), as well as place names such as Väderstad ('windy town'). *Väder* might also be used to refer to flatulence, with the expression *släppa väder* meaning 'to break wind'.

So what about that *o*?

The prefix *o* is most often used in Swedish as a form of negation for adjectives, adverbs, verbs and nouns, similar to the English prefix 'un-'.

For example, *rimlig* ('reasonable') becomes *orimlig* ('unreasonable'), *lycklig* ('happy') becomes *olycklig* ('unhappy'), *en möjlighet* ('a possibility') becomes *en omöjlighet* ('an impossibility'), and *gjord* ('done') becomes *ogjord* ('undone or unfinished').

The prefix *o* as a negation is especially common in the Norrland region, where it's used in many more instances than it is in the rest of the country.

For example, in Norrland speech, *o* can be added to adjectives such as *bra* to create *obra* ('not good'), but most Swedes would say *dålig*, 'bad', or simply *inte bra*.

O can also be used in standard Swedish as a prefix to denote an abnormal, extreme form of the root noun, implying judgment from the speaker. For example, the word *odjur* means 'beast' or 'monster', from *o* + *djur* ('animal'), while *ogräs* (*o* + *gräs*, literally 'un-grass') means 'weed', referring to undesirable plants, and *ovän* (*o* + *vän*, 'friend') doesn't simply mean someone who is not your friend, but someone who is an enemy.

If it feels confusing, the English language does the same thing in some specific contexts: think of how 'undead' doesn't mean something that is alive, but a paranormal being that acts like it's alive.

Oväder falls into this category: it doesn't refer to a lack of weather but rather weather that is unusual and extreme. Weather so unpleasant isn't worthy of the name 'weather'.

There should be some form of precipitation to classify as *oväder*, either snow, rain, or hail, and it usually indicates winds as well, but there is no official meteorological definition.

You could use it in phrases like *ett tillfälligt oväder* ('a temporary storm') or *Vilket oväder vi har fått* ('What bad weather we've had').

Inställda tåg på grund av oväder.
Cancelled trains due to extreme weather/storms.

Nytt oväder på väg in över hela Sverige.
Another storm/instance of extreme weather is on its way across all of Sweden.

An un-Swedish un-friend

The Swedish *o* suffix mostly works as a negation, but sometimes it makes the word take on a new meaning.

ett odjur	'un-animal'	a monster
(ett) ogräs	'un-grass'	weed
osvensk	'un-Swedish'	cheerful and sociable

How would you translate the following words to 'real' English?

(ett) oljud	'un-sound'
(en) oordning	'un-order'
(en) oro	'un-calmness'
(en) otur	'un-luck'
ett oväder	'un-weather'
en ovän	'un-friend'

oljud = noise ◊ *oordning* = mess ◊ *oro* = (a) worry ◊ *otur* = bad luck ◊ *oväder* = storm ◊ *ovän* = enemy

Polkagris **'Candy cane'** NOUN

pɔl:kagri:s

The *polkagris* is a roll of peppermint flavoured, usually red and white striped candy in the shape of a stick or a hook.

The sweets were invented by Swedish confectioner Amalia Eriksson in the town of Gränna in 1859, and today, as in other countries, they are enjoyed year round as well as being used to decorate Christmas trees.

The *polka* in the name comes directly from the dance, polka.

At the time this fast-paced Slavic dance was a new thing in Scandinavia, and it was used in the name *polkagris* because of the fast candy-twirling action needed to roll the red and white sections together before the sugar sets to give the stick its distinctive swirls.

As for *gris*, this literally means 'pig', but was a common slang term for candy or sweets in the 1800s.

You'll also hear the sweets referred to as *polkakäpp*, especially when the end is curved round into a hook (to be hung on a tree), from *käpp* meaning 'walking stick'.

This is a more generic term, whereas *polkagris* usually refers to sweets made with Eriksson's precise methods and secret recipe. This was closely guarded, and the first shop making authentic *polkagrisar* outside Gränna opened as recently as 2011. Today it is also made in the Swedish Candy Factory in California.

And today you can also find a huge variety of flavours of *polkagrisar*, from the traditional peppermint to the more original apple, mojito, or caramel, to name just a few.

Polkagrisar kan hängas upp som julpynt.
Candy sticks can be hung up as Christmas decorations.

Chokladtryffel med smak av polkagris.
Chocolate truffle flavoured with candy cane (peppermint).

Prosit 'Bless you' INTERJECTION

pɾuːsɪt

Prosit is the standard Swedish response when someone sneezes.

It comes from the Latin word *prosit*, which means something like 'may it be good', from the verb *prosum*. You can translate it as 'bless you'.

There are several different theories about why we bless people after sneezing, but one possibility is it's because sneezes were thought to be due to interference from good or evil spirits, so a blessing was intended to ward off potentially evil spirits.

Another story goes that centuries ago, people believed your heart stopped momentarily when you sneezed, while others still say that the expression originated during the plague, when people blessed sneezing friends in a bid to ward off the mysterious sickness.

Whatever the answer, most Swedes will respond to a sneeze with a thoughtful *prosit* — and it's the same in Danish and Norwegian, too.

In many cultures, people respond to sneezes by either saying 'bless you' or 'good health'. In German, for example, the usual response to sneezing is *Gesundheit!* (literally 'health' with the understood meaning of 'I wish you good health') while *Prost!* also deriving from Latin *prosit* is used as a toast when drinking.

The late Swedish etiquette expert Magdalena Ribbing noted that it is polite to say *prosit* the first time someone sneezes, but that if they're caught in a sneezing attack, you don't need to keep repeating it. Beware though: Swedish folklore dictates that each time you say *tack* (thank you) in response to *prosit,* a gnome will die.

Atjo! Prosit!
Achoo! Bless you!

På svenska brukar vi säga "prosit" när någon nyser.
In Swedish we usually say '*prosit*' when someone sneezes.

Puss **'Kiss'; 'peck'** NOUN

pɵsː

A *puss* is a specific type of kiss: usually brief and with a closed mouth, equivalent to English 'peck'. It doesn't have to be romantic or sexual. You'll hear people say it to their friends and family members as much as, if not more than, to their partners.

Puss puss ('kiss kiss') is a common way of saying 'goodbye' between friends, like a verbal version of the French or Italian cheek kiss greeting, and you can say *tusen pussar* ('a thousand kisses') for closer relationships such as between siblings, parents and children, and good friends.

Puss can also be used as a verb: *pussa*, as in *Hon pussade honom på kinden* ('She kissed him on the cheek').

If you want to talk about a more romantic or passionate kiss, that's *en kyss*. Be warned: the verb *att kyssa* may be linguistically related to the English 'kiss', but *kissa* in Swedish means 'to pee'. So make sure to pronounce *kyssa* with a soft *k* (similar to the English 'sh') to avoid any awkward misunderstandings.

You might be wondering if there's any link to the English word 'puss', a slang term for cat, which is related to *poes* in Dutch, *Puus* in Low German, and *pus* in Norwegian. The etymology of these words isn't known for sure, but it's possible that they actually share a root with Swedish *puss*.

The Local put the question to Sweden's Language Council,

which told us: "The Swedish dictionary says that *puss* is recorded in Swedish since 1712 and comes from the Swedish dialect word *puss*, probably onomatopoeically."

They were unable to comment on any connection between English and Swedish *puss*, but in both English and German, 'puss' was originally the name used for calling a cat. In modern Irish, *pus* means mouth, and can be used in particular to describe a sulky look with pursed lips or a pout. Therefore it's possible that all of these words share a root which described a pouting expression, which was likened to the call for a cat in many languages but to a kiss in Swedish.

And interestingly, the Swedish equivalent of 'pussycat' is *kissekatt* or simply *kisse*.

Puss och kram!
Hugs and kisses!*

Hon pussade sin lille son på pannan.
She kissed her little boy on the forehead.

---

* A common way to say 'goodbye'.

Påskris 'Easter twigs' NOUN

pɔsːkɾiːs

Påskris is a term that many initially mistranslate as 'Easter rice', but it actually means 'Easter branches/twigs'.

The first part of the word is the easiest to trace through history: *påsk* means 'Easter'. It is etymologically linked to Jewish Passover, both sharing roots in the Hebrew word *pesaḥ* which meant 'to pass over', which became *pascha* in Latin and *páskar* in Old Norse before transforming into *påsk* in modern Swedish.

You can use it on its own in expressions like *Glad påsk!* ('Happy Easter!') and *vid påsk* ('at Easter time'), but just like the word *jul* ('Christmas'), it is also used in plenty of festive compound words, and *påskris* is one of the most important.

If you've learned Swedish food vocabulary, you'll probably know that *ris* means 'rice', but it can also mean 'rod', either literally ('a stick') or figuratively. Similar to the English phrase 'carrot and stick' referring to encouragement through both rewards and punishment, the Swedish phrase *ris och ros* (literally 'rod and rose') means 'criticism and praise'.

In the word *påskris*, ris means 'rod' in the literal sense.

Back in the 1600s, Swedes used to beat each other with sticks and rods on Good Friday, as a way of remembering Jesus' suffering and experiencing suffering themselves. If you're from an eastern European country such as the Czech Republic, you might recognise this tradition. The rods were called *fastlagsris* (literally 'Lent rods').

Luckily, this is no longer the typical way of marking Easter, and these days sticks are used as pretty decorations rather than whips. This tradition started around the Stockholm area in the late 1800s, and became common across the whole country by the 1930s.

So *påskris* are twigs, often from birch, which are used to decorate inside and outside the home during the Easter celebrations, almost like a springtime variant on the Christmas tree.

In the religious context, it might symbolise the palm leaves said to have been scattered in front of Jesus when he entered Jerusalem on the Sunday before Easter. But in secular Sweden, they're also just a way of adding colour and greenery to homes around March and April.

You'll see the twigs, topped with colourful feathers, on sale at markets and other shops in the lead-up to Easter, although in recent years, the use of real feathers has declined, due to concerns for animal welfare.

You can add extra decorations to your twigs, such as hanging eggs or animal-themed ornaments.

However you display them, *påskris* are an important and beautiful part of the Easter festivities in Sweden.

Jag vill ha påskris utan fjädrar.
I want to have Easter branches without feathers.

Påskriset ser underbart ut!
The Easter branches look wonderful!

Påtår 'Refill (of coffee)' NOUN

poːtoːr

Påtår is almost exclusively used to refer to coffee. So when you've emptied your cup of *bryggkaffe* ('filter coffee', the standard at most Swedish cafes) and want another mug-full, you ask for *en påtår*.

You'll often see it included on menus: *påtår — 5 kronor* or similar, and if you're a big coffee-drinker, it's well worth your while to find a cafe that offers cheap or even free *påtår*.

It won't always be on the price list though. Often, if the coffeepot is accessible to customers, it's a sign that it's OK to give yourself a refill but if you're unsure, just ask. *Ingår påtår?* is how you ask 'Are refills included?' A great sentence for practising the beautiful Swedish *å* sound.

You can also use *påtår* outside cafes, for example if your friends are visiting you at home. Once their mugs are empty, show off both your Swedish and your hosting skills by asking *Påtår?*

This word dates back to at least 1842, when the first recorded use of *påtår* is found. It's not often used for other beverages, so if you want a refill or second cup of a non-caffeinated drink, say either *Påfyllning, tack* ('A refill, please') or *En till, tack* ('Another please' — you might need to point at your glass to be clear what you want a second serving of).

Påtår comes from the outdated word *kaffetår*, which in the

1800s was used to refer to the first cup of coffee. *Tår* means 'tear', as in when you cry, but it used to mean a 'drop' or a 'sip' of a drink, and in fact it is still used in that way in Danish. So *en kaffetår* meant 'a drop of coffee'.

På is a preposition with a wide range of meanings, most often translated as 'on'. It comes from the Old Norse word *upp á*, which also gave us the English word 'upon' (and English 'up' and Swedish *upp* as well as *på*). The word *fylla på* means 'to refill/replenish/fill up', and so *en påtår* meant 'another *kaffetår*'.

The Swedes didn't stop there.

According to the Swedish Academy's dictionary, there used to be a special word for the third consecutive cup of coffee, *tretår*, from *tre* ('three'). A fourth cup was *en krusetår* (from *krusa* meaning 'to insist'), and the rarely used term for the fifth cup was *en pintår* (from the noun *pina* meaning misery or torment).

Now, the word *kaffetår* and the other variations have almost entirely dropped out of use, so when ordering your first cup you say *En kopp kaffe, tack* ('A cup of coffee, please'), *En bryggkaffe, tack* ('A filter coffee, please') or similar.

Vill du ha påtår?
Do you want a refill?

De sitter och dricker påtår på påtår.
They are drinking coffee after coffee.

Raggmunk **'Potato pancake'** NOUN

ɾag:mɵŋ:k

Raggmunk literally means 'hairy monk', but more commonly it's the name for a potato pancake, a traditional hearty Swedish winter dish.

You see, *ragg* comes from the Old Norse word *rögg*, which referred to a tuft or a bit of wool. In Swedish *ragg* was used to describe coarse fur, hair or wool, usually belonging to an animal — Swedish also has the adjective *raggig*, meaning 'bushy/shaggy/matted/crisp'.

Ragg can be used as a slang term to describe someone you're having a casual relationship with too, in which case it's a noun: *ett ragg* ('a hook-up'). The verb *ragga*, and sometimes *ragga upp* can mean 'to flirt with', for example: *Han raggar upp tjejer på krogen* ('He chats up girls at the pub'). But that doesn't have anything to do with our potato pancakes.

Like *ragg*, *munk* also has two meanings. It can refer to monks in the religious sense, and has its roots in the Latin term *monachus* ('monk') which was borrowed into old Germanic languages.

Munk can also mean 'doughnut' — the two different meanings are actually related, because ring doughnuts were thought to look a bit like the traditional monks' haircut which involved shaving most of their head to leave a ring of hair.

Swedish *raggmunkar* are often cooked in a *munkpanna*, and

should be *raggig* in the sense of 'crisp' when they're ready, hence the name.

The Swedish potato pancake was first created around the early 1900s, according to Sweden's *Raggmunk* Academy, and is still enjoyed today, often with pork and lingonberries.

Raggmunk med fläsk är en traditionell svensk maträtt.
Potato pancake with pork is a traditional Swedish meal.

Jag väljer alltid raggmunk när det finns på menyn.
I always choose potato pancake when it's on the menu.

Fried chicken is alive

Swedish is known for its compound words. But what happens when you don't combine them the right way? Depending on whether the words are written together or apart they take different meanings:

giftorm	venomous snake
gift orm	married snake
ätpinnar	chopsticks
ät pinnar	eat sticks!
sjukgymnast	physiotherapist
sjuk gymnast	[a] sick gymnast
herrtoalett	men's bathroom
herr toalett	Mister Toilet
ringmunk	ring doughnut
ring munk	call [a] monk!
renkorv	reindeer sausage
ren korv	clean sausage
stekt kycklinglever	fried chicken liver
stekt kyckling lever	fried chicken is alive

Rolig 'Fun'; 'funny', 'entertaining' NOUN

ɾuːlɪ

Rolig is used to mean any one of the following: 'fun', 'funny', 'entertaining', 'interesting'. You can use *rolig* to describe people, objects, experiences and much more — anything which brings a smile to your face. You can also use it in the sense of 'funny' meaning 'odd', so *en rolig liten gubbe* might refer to a funny-looking man, rather than one with a humorous personality — you'd have to rely on tone to work out which meaning was intended.

You'll also hear it in the set phrase *att ha (det) roligt* ('to have fun/to have a good time').

The history of the word *rolig* is packed with linguistic twists and turns. It's been used by Swedish speakers since at least 1655, when it appeared in the Swedish translation of the Bible.

But back then, *rolig* meant 'calm' or 'quiet', almost the opposite of today's meaning. And it is used in present-day Danish and Norwegian to mean 'calm' too, so that a Dane and a Swede might end up confused and disappointed if one invites the other for *en rolig helg* ('a fun/quiet weekend', depending on who's speaking).

Words often change their meaning over time, sometimes to reflect changes in society and how people live, sometimes to fill a gap in the lexicon, and sometimes for no clear reason at all.

This process tends to happen most often and most quickly with adjectives. Sometimes an adjective is used so much that its meaning is weakened, or it is used so often in a certain context that it takes on a narrower connotation than it earlier had.

In the case of *rolig*, the original usage in the sense of 'calm/quiet' tended to have a positive connotation, so over time it came to be used to mean 'pleasant' more generally. In recent decades, its meaning has grown stronger, so that it is closer to 'fun' or *kul* than 'nice' or *trevlig*.

This helps explain why *rolig*'s apparent opposite, *orolig*, means 'anxious/worried' rather than 'not fun'. And there are other traces in Swedish of the older meaning. The noun *ro*, the root of *rolig*, still means 'peace/tranquility' and is used in the phrase *lugn och ro* ('peace and quiet').

Ha det så roligt!
Have fun/have a nice time!

Han är inte så rolig att leva med.
He isn't that easy to live with.

Rötmånad 'The month when fresh food goes off quickly' NOUN

ɾøːtmoːnad

Rötmånad literally means 'rotting month', from the noun *röta* ('rot') and *månad* ('month').

It's used to describe the period from late July to late August. Some people might say it runs from July 23rd to August 23rd, but others use it to talk about any part of the summer with high temperatures and humidity which might cause fresh food to go off more quickly.

It's much less of a worry since the invention of fridges, but the Swedish Food Agency still issues advice to use cooler bags for picnics and to store and transport food appropriately during this time of year. Taking these precautions, particularly with raw meat, helps to avoid unnecessary food waste and bacteria-borne illnesses.

You can also translate *rötmånad* into English as 'dog days', a term to refer to the days of late summer where the long, humid days were thought to lead to bad luck and mysterious happenings, such as sudden thunderstorms and food deteriorating in quality. Of course, these days we know there are scientific reasons as to why these things happen on summer days.

A *rötmånadshistoria* (literally 'rotting month story' or 'dog days story') is a term to refer to stories with fantastic and unbelievable elements, because of an association between this time of year and unusual events.

And, according to superstition, calves with deformities were more likely to be born in this late summer period, so they are sometimes called *rötmånadskalv* (literally 'a dog days calf').

Augusti är känd som rötmånaden.
August is known as the 'rotting month'.

När det är rötmånad får man ha extra koll på maten så att den inte blir dålig.
In the dog days of summer, you have to keep an extra eye on your food so it doesn't go bad.

Semester 'Holiday' NOUN

sɛmɛsːtɛr

This word might mean the exact opposite of what you'd expect.

Semester means 'holiday' or 'vacation' in Swedish, but only referring to time off work (time off school is called *lov*).

It's a pretty crucial word in Sweden, where full-time workers are entitled to at least 25 days of holiday by law, and up to four weeks of that can usually be taken consecutively during the summer.

The related verb *semestra* means 'to go on holiday', for example *Vi ska semestra i Sverige i år* ('We're going to go on holiday in Sweden this year'). You can also use the phrase *åka på semester* instead.

So why is the meaning different from English 'semester', referring to a term of education?

Well, in Latin, *semestris* meant 'six-month', coming from *sex* ('six') and *mensis* ('month', from the word for 'moon'). It entered English and French through German as a word for a university or school term, as these were split into two units within a year; six months each.

In Swedish, though, *semester* has been used since the 18th century to refer to holidays, originally linked specifically to army officers, who had the right to a certain amount of vacation. The Swedish word for a term of education is *termin*.

You can find the word *semester* in several compound nouns, such as *campingsemester* ('camping holiday'), *semesterö* ('holiday island') or *semestertillägg* ('holiday supplement', the extra pay workers in Sweden receive when they take annual leave as part of the country's vacation law).

And the recently coined portmanteau *hemester* (*hem* or 'home' + *semester*) is the equivalent of the English term 'staycation' to refer to a holiday within one's country of residence. Less commonly, you'll hear *svemester* (from *Sverige* or 'Sweden' + *semester*), which means the same thing within Sweden.

Jag behöver semester!
I need a holiday!

Vi tog en månads semester.
We took a month off work.

Skog **'Forest'** NOUN

sku:g

More than half of Sweden — an area equal to the size of the United Kingdom — is covered in trees. This area is growing thanks to protective policies that mean the growth rate outpaces the felling rate. And these forests provide around ten percent of Swedish employment and exports, everything from furniture to toilet paper.

Most of Sweden's forests are owned either privately or by companies, but the Swedish Constitution grants everyone the so-called right to roam, meaning everyone can hike, camp, and pick berries in nature. And they do. Spending time in the forest is a big part of the Swedish lifestyle, whether holidaying in a remote *stuga* (cabin) or on a day out hunting for mushrooms.

The old Swedish word *skogher* is the root of today's *skog*; initially it meant 'something that protrudes' — think of the trees protruding from the ground.

The word *skog* is also used in several common phrases. Despite the Swedish love for forests, these are usually negative.

The most common is *Dra åt skogen!*, literally 'Go to the forest!' but used as a slightly politer version of 'Go to hell!'.

When a project 'goes to the forest' (*går åt skogen*) it means it's gone wrong.

And you can say someone or something is *skogstokig* (literally 'forest crazy') meaning 'totally crazy'.

Jag tog en lugn skogspromenad.
I went for a calm walk in the forest.

Här är bara skog överallt.
Around here there's nothing but forest.

Skål **'Cheers'** NOUN/INTERJECTION

<u>sko:l</u>

Skål means two different things in Swedish, and they're both common words. *En skål* is 'a bowl' and *skål* is how you say 'cheers!' — the exclamation when you clink glasses with friends and drink, often in celebration of something. Except in Sweden, you shouldn't let your glasses touch.

Sweden has some fairly complex etiquette when it comes to toasting. At formal occasions, there's a set order in which you should toast the people you're with, and you should raise your glass to the third button on your shirt.

But in general, unless you're keeping very fancy company, all you need to remember to avoid offence is to make eye contact and nod at your cheers-ing partner.

The usual preposition you use with *skål* is *för*, for example *Skål för vänskap!* ('Cheers to friendship!') or *Skål för Ayda!* ('Cheers to Ayda!'), but you can also say *Skål på dig!* ('Cheers to you!').

You can turn skål into a verb too, *skåla* ('to toast, or to drink to'), as in: *Ska vi skåla för det?* ('Shall we drink to that?'), and the noun *en skål* is 'a toast'.

As for where the word comes from, it's slightly related to *skål*'s other meaning of 'bowl'. *Skål* meaning 'cheers' comes from the word *skal* meaning 'shell' or 'outer covering'. In older forms of Swedish, this word was used to refer to drinking vessels.

Jag vill utbringa en skål för det lyckliga paret.
I'd like to propose a toast to the happy couple.

Skål för det!
Cheers to that!

Details that matter

The three extra vowels of Swedish are a serious matter. These dots and rings are not decoration only, but serve an important purpose. For example, *skål* ('bowl', or 'cheers') without the ring makes *skal*, 'a shell' or 'a peel'.

Med vänliga hälsningar.	Kind regards.
Med vanliga halsningar.	Common swigs.
Vilken vacker röst.	What a beautiful voice.
Vilken vacker rost.	What beautiful rust.
Vi har en gäst hemma.	We have a guest at home.
Vi har en gast hemma.	We have a ghost at home.
Jag älskar far.	I love [my] father.
Jag älskar får.	I love sheep.
Man får inte svära!	You are not allowed to curse!
Man får inte svara!	You are not allowed to reply!
Trevligt att råkas.	Nice to meet you.
Trevligt att rakas.	Nice to be shaved.
Jag glömde min sjal hemma.	I left my scarf at home.
Jag glömde min själ hemma.	I left my soul at home.
Förstår du?	Do you understand?
Förstör du?	Do you destroy?
Hon har verkligen humor.	She really has a good sense of humour.
Hon har verkligen humör.	She is really moody.

Smörgås 'Sandwich' NOUN

smœr:gɔs

Smörgås is most familiar to non-Swedish speakers as part of the compound noun *smörgåsbord* (literally 'sandwich table' but in practice a buffet of different dishes.) In English it's usually used to mean 'a wide variety'.

In fact, a Swedish *smörgås* wouldn't really be defined as a 'sandwich' at all in English, where the most defining characteristic of a sandwich is that the filling is placed between two slices of bread. A Swedish *smörgås* is usually one slice of bread, with butter and a topping — perhaps meat, vegetables, or cheese — placed on top. You can use the word *dubbelsmörgås* ('double sandwich') to describe a sandwich featuring two slices of bread.

So what makes a *smörgås* a *smörgås*? *Smör* means 'butter', which is spread on the bread before the other ingredients go on top. *Gås* on its own means 'goose', but it's uncertain what these have got to do with Swedish sandwiches.

Instead of 'skimming/skipping stones' (throwing pebbles across a water's surface), Swedes *kastar smörgås* ('throw a sandwich'). A *smörgåstårta* ('sandwich cake') is exactly what it sounds like: sandwich ingredients, layered and decorated just like a dessert cake, except it's cold, savoury and often fishy.

There are other words for 'sandwich', most commonly *macka*, thought to come from the Romani word *mak* ('bread') or possibly the German verb *machen* ('to make'), which is used more often when talking about heated sandwiches (*varma mackor*). The Swedish word for 'toast' is *rostat bröd* ('roasted bread').

Han hade en smörgås i handen.
He had a sandwich in his hand.

Jag har ätit upp min smörgås.
I ate up my sandwich.

Literal compound words

Swedish compound words often take a literal approach to understanding the world:

dammsugare	**'dust sucker'**	vacuum cleaner
glasögon	**'glass eyes'**	glasses
uppehållsväder	**'interruption weather'**	sunny

How would you translate the following words to 'real' English?

bröstvårta	**'breast wart'**
fladdermus	**'flutter mouse'**
flodhäst	**'river horse'**
grönsak	**'green thing'**
moderkaka	**'mother cookie'**
munspel	**'mouth play'**
sjukhus	**'sick house'**
sköldpadda	**'shield toad'**
sugrör	**'suck pipe'**
tandkött	**'tooth meat'**

bröstvårta = nipple ◇ *fladdermus* = bat ◇ *flodhäst* = hippo ◇ *grönsak* = vegetable
◇ *moderkaka* = placenta ◇ *munspel* = harmonica ◇ *sjukhus* = hospital
◇ *sköldpadda* = turtle/tortoise ◇ *sugrör* = straw ◇ *tandkött* = gums

Snapsvisa 'Traditional drinking song' NOUN

snap:svi:sa

The first half of this word is easy to decipher. *Snaps* is a Scandinavian spirit (related to German *Schnapps* linguistically, but not quite the same) often drunk with a meal on special occasions. It has been made in Sweden since the Middle Ages when monks produced the alcohol for medicinal use.

Snaps is extremely strong, served chilled and unmixed, often in a special glass that looks a bit like a long shot glass. It comes in several varieties — traditional *snaps*, called aquavit, is flavoured with dill and cumin seeds, and these days you'll find varieties flavoured with all kinds of berries, fruits and other herbs.

En visa meanwhile means 'song'. The usual Swedish words for 'song' are *en låt* or *en sång*, but the older word *visa* has survived in some set phrases and compound nouns like *snapsvisa*, 'snaps song'.

The *snapsvisor* or 'drinking songs' are uniquely Swedish. They are thought to have originated around a century ago, probably with their roots in student drinking culture, but today are enjoyed by adults of all ages, so don't be surprised to see your grandparents-in-law singing along with the youngsters at the *julbord* ('Christmas meal').

More than 10,000 different drinking songs have been recorded in Sweden, according to the *Spritmuseum* (Spirit Museum) in

Stockholm, which each year organises a competition for new drinking songs to help keep the tradition thriving. They are sung at all kinds of festivities that feature snaps, from Christmas to Midsummer to birthday and graduation parties.

Alla vid julbordet började sjunga snapsvisor.
Everyone started to sing drinking songs at the Christmas buffet.

Helan går *är en klassisk snapsvisa.*
Helan går is a classic drinking song.

Snömos 'Words without meaning' NOUN

snø:mu:s

Snömos looks like a weather word, but it's usually talking about something quite different.

Snö means 'snow', and *mos* means 'pulp' or 'mash' (*potatismos* means 'mashed potatoes'), so it sounds like a word for either fluffy snow or slush.

But this word is usually used in a metaphorical sense.

If you say that someone is serving or producing *snömos*, it means they are talking with beautiful imagery or powerful ideas, but no substance.

It's often used about politicians who offer plenty of rhetoric but less concrete options, or you might use it about a boss who talks about company values that are rarely acted upon, an article that fails to get to the point, or anyone else who uses meaningless phrases or empty promises. The idea behind this image is that the words are similar to fluffy fallen snow: they will soon melt to nothing.

Hon lovade mycket, men det var bara en massa snömos.
She promised a lot, but it was just a load of empty talk.

Som vanligt var det bara snömos på presskonferensen.
As usual, there was only empty talk at the press conference.

Different words for snow

Language reflects reality, and Sweden experiences long and cold winters, meaning there are plenty of words for snow. Below we have a few:

nysnö	new snow
blötsnö	wet snow
pudersnö	powder snow
snökanon	lake-effect snow
knarrsnö	squeaky snow
kramsnö	'squeeze snow', the right consistency for making snowballs
snöblandat regn	'snow-mixed rain' — sleet
slask	slush or partly melted snow
snösörja	another word for slush
modd	slush mixed with dirt
skare	the crust on packed snow when one layer melts and then freezes over again
dagsmeja	snow melting in the sunshine

The Sami languages, spoken by the indigenous Sami people of northern Sweden, can add even more. By some counts, there are over 200 snow words in the languages, some of them very technical and used by reindeer herders.

muohta	snow in general
habllek	powder snow
soavli	slushy snow
vahca	new snow
ciegar	a snowfield that has been trampled by reindeer

Spissflabbad 'Pointy-mouthed' (Skåne dialect)

ADJECTIVE

spɪs:flab:ad

Skåningar or 'Scanians', as people from Sweden's southern county, Skåne, are called, tend not to have a high opinion of anyone from *uppåt landet* ('up the country'). Their preferred term for the way such hoity-toity northerners speak is *spissflabbad.*

Spissflabbad literally means pointy-mouthed (*spiss* comes from the Swedish word *spetsig* and *flabb* is a dialect word for 'mouth') and to be *spissflabbad* is to speak in an overly refined, posh and affected way.

Someone born and bred in the upmarket Stockholm district of Östermalm would certainly be *spissflabbad*, but so too would almost anyone from anywhere north of Helsingborg without a strong working-class accent.

The term has its origins in the differences between how Scanians and most other Swedes speak.

If you've ever tried to get your mouth (or perhaps throat) around the Scanian *r*, you will know that it is voiced right at the back of the tongue, like in Danish or northern French dialects (it is either an 'uvular trill' or an 'uvular fricative').

Pulling off Scanian's sharp diphthongs also requires considerable movement from the speaker's mouth.

So to a Scanian, the central Swedish accent spoken in

Stockholm, Uppsala, Eskilstuna and Västerås, sounds like it is spoken right on the tip of the tongue, with little discernible movement of the mouth and lips.

The term is also, indeed perhaps most often, used to refer to other Scanians who have somewhat softened their accent, either as a result of living elsewhere or gaining an education.

Du har tappat din dialekt och blivit spissflabbad sedan du flyttade till Stockholm.
You have lost your accent and become 'pointy-mouthed' since you moved to Stockholm.

Pratar du långt bak i munnen eller är du spissflabbad?
Do you speak from the back of your mouth or are you pointy-mouthed?

Stuga 'Cabin' NOUN

stʉ:ga

Stuga is most commonly used to describe a small dwelling: smaller than the average house, often someone's holiday home or second home, and it could be translated into English as 'cabin' or 'cottage'.

It's often used in the compound noun *sommarstuga* to refer to the many summer cabins that dot Sweden's coastlines, forests and islands and serve as a holiday escape for many families.

But their use isn't limited to summer and Swedes often also host their families there for celebrations at other times of the year, including over Christmas — usually only if their *stuga* is heated though, which isn't always the case. Many of these cottages don't have electricity or running water, but you'll also find fancier *stugor* with all the mod cons you could wish for.

The word *stuga* conjures up lots of evocative feelings for Swedes. These are typically places of peace, comfort, and *mys* or 'cosiness', much closer to nature than city apartments.

The word is also sometimes used to describe a room, often one with a specific purpose: a *tvättstuga* ('laundry room') might be a separate building but can also be used to talk about a room in a house, a *förstuga* (most often shortened to *farstu*) is a porch or hall, and *bastu* ('sauna') is a shortening of *badstuga* meaning 'bathing room'.

The word *stuga* comes from the Old Swedish word *stuva* and has several linguistic relations: Icelandic *stofa* means 'living room' as does Norwegian *stue*, and English 'stove' (which earlier meant 'heated room' and only later came to refer to one of the devices that did the heating) is also from the same root. While these words refer to different parts of the house, they all retain the connotation of warmth at home.

Vi har en liten stuga i skogen.
We have a little cottage in the woods.

Hon hade alltid drömt om att bygga en egen stuga.
Her dream was to build a cottage of her own.

Surströmming **'Fermented herring'** NOUN

sʉːʂʈʂœmːɪŋ

Surströmming has been a traditional (and smelly) part of Swedish cuisine for centuries. One of the most putrid-smelling foods in the world, eating this delicacy is one of the final frontiers for proving you've adapted to the Swedish palate.

It's a controversial food to say the least, with several airlines banning the carriage of *surströmming*, and viral challenges where people film their first attempt eating the fish.

Sur means 'sour' or 'fermented' and relates both to the acidic taste and the method of preparation. To prepare *surströmming*, fish caught at the start of the season are preserved with salt to stop them rotting.

The process takes about six months, so the first date on which you can eat *surströmming* is known as the *surströmmingspremiär*, traditionally the third Thursday in August.

There are guidelines on how best to eat the dish, the most important of which is to try it outdoors due to the odour. The traditional way to serve it is with onion, sour cream, bread, potatoes and a glass of snaps — not straight out of the can.

Most languages find one word for 'herring' is sufficient, but in Sweden there's a difference between herring caught south of the Kalmar Strait, which are *sill*, and those caught in the Baltic north of Kalmar, which are *strömming*.

The differentiation started after a royal request in the 16th century which established the boundary, but whether the fish are actually different is up for debate. Generally, *sill* are larger and fattier than *strömming*, and some research suggests there are slight genetic differences, despite being part of the same species and very closely related.

Jag äter det mesta, till och med surströmming.
I eat most things, even fermented herring.

Många i Sverige har som tradition att äta surströmming varje sommar.
For many people in Sweden it's a tradition to eat fermented herring every summer.

Sverige 'Sweden' NOUN

sfæɾ:jɛ

The names we use for countries tell us a lot about their history. In the case of Sweden, we can trace the name back to at least the 13th century, when it was called *Swerike* in Old Swedish.

Sverige can be broken down into two parts. The second part of the word Sverige comes from the noun *rike* ('realm' or 'kingdom'). You'll also see this word in *riksdag*, the name for the country's parliament.

As for the *Sve-*, most people believe this came from the term *svear*, the name of a tribe called 'the Swedes' in English.

The *svear* lived in the central part of what is now Sweden, roughly corresponding to the region now called Svealand, the middle of Sweden's three core regions. Meanwhile, the tribe known as the *götar* ('Geats' in English) inhabited the southern region known as Götaland today. The third, northern region is Norrland.

Some linguists and historians have argued that the *sve* in *Sverige* comes from an older Indo-European word meaning 'our/us', and that *Sverige* literally means 'our kingdom'. According to this theory, the *götar* and *svear* may have chosen this name together as a neutral name for their combined countries.

During the 13th century, *Swerike* became *Svearike*, and by the 16th century it became *Swerighe*, although there were alternative spellings including *Swerghe* and *Swirghe*.

You'll see *Sverige* used in a few compound words, such as *Sverigebo* ('Swedish resident') or *Sverigevän* ('friend of Sweden', which used to refer to foreign-born people with a strong interest in the country, but in recent years has acquired nationalistic connotations).

Sverige är fantastiskt!
Sweden is wonderful!

Jag flyttade till Sverige för två år sedan.
I moved to Sweden two years ago.

Sambo & särbo 'A person who lives with their partner' & 'a person who lives apart from their partner' NOUN

sam:bʊ sæ:ɾbʊ

These are two words to describe people in different living situations.

Sambo is a shortening of *sammanboende*, meaning 'cohabiting partner' or literally 'together-living', which is used for couples who share a household but are unmarried. It's a legal status, but you could also refer to *min sambo* in the same way you'd say 'my partner/girlfriend/boyfriend'.

Särbo is the equivalent for couples who do not live together. *Särbo* is a combination of *isär* ('apart') and *boende* ('living').

Särbo was first used in the 1980s, some years after *sambo* entered common usage.

Another term in the same category is the more colloquial or jokey term *mambo*, which translates as 'living with mum' (*mamma* in Swedish) and is used to talk about people, usually single, who live with their parents into adulthood.

Särbo has connotations of a serious, long-term relationship, rather than someone you've only been dating casually or for a short amount of time. If you're not confident you've reached that level, it's better to use a term like *flickvän/pojkvän* ('girlfriend/boyfriend') until you have that talk.

Min sambo har en syster.
My partner (who lives with me) has a sister.

Peter och Julia är särbo.
Peter and Julia are in a relationship and live apart.

The way we live now

Swedish has many words for different relationships and living arrangements, all based on *bo* — to live in the sense of inhabit.

sambo *tillsammans* — together	**someone you live with but haven't married**
särbo *isär* — separate	**someone you are in a long-term relationship with but don't live with**
mambo *mamma* — mother	**someone who (involuntarily) lives with their parents**
kombo *kompis* — friend	**someone who lives with a friend (although this is unusual)**
iblandbo *ibland* — sometimes	**someone you live with once in a while but haven't married**
smygbo *smyga* — sneak	**someone who lives with a friend but needs to sneak in and out in secret**
hambo *hamster* — hamster	**lives with their hamster**
exbo *ex* — ex	**newly divorced but still living together**

All but one of these expressions are used more or less frequently. Which one does not describe a conventional living arrangement?

Tjej **'Girl'** NOUN

ɕɛjː

Tjej is a word that Swedish took from the Romani language decades ago.

It refers to a young woman or to somebody's girlfriend (much like the male equivalent, *kille*). It can also be used in compound nouns, for example *tjejkväll* ('girls' night'), *tjejmilen* (the name of an annual women's running competition in Stockholm) or *hästtjej* ('a girl who really likes horses').

This word comes from Scandoromani, the language of the North Germanic Romani people, where it means 'daughter' and is spelled *čhai*, the female version of *čhavo*, 'boy'.

The Swedish Academy dictionary dates it back to 1851, but when it was first incorporated into Swedish slang, the term was used to refer to young working class women. It then morphed into a term for teenage girls, before taking on a more general meaning for a young woman.

An article from the *Dagens Nyheter* newspaper in 1929 recommended that "in a children's novel" it is preferable to speak of *an ungmö* ('young maiden') or *flicka* ('girl') rather than a *tjej*. Today, the word is commonly used by most Swedes and is not considered to be vulgar slang.

There is no clear line demarcating when someone ceases to be a *tjej* and becomes a *kvinna* ('woman') and feminist debates sometimes criticise when adult women are referred to, or refer to themselves, as *tjejer* when men of the same age would be called *män* ('men') and not *killar*.

> ***Jag och min tjej har köpt hus.***
> My girlfriend and I have bought a house.
>
> ***Hej, tjejer!***
> Hi, gals!

Minority languages of Sweden

Did you know there are five official minority languages in Sweden?

Finnish There are between 500,000 and 1 million Sweden Finns in the country, mainly in Stockholm and the Mälaren Valley. Unlike Norwegian and Danish, Finnish comes from an entirely different language family to Swedish.

Meänkieli/Tornedale Finnish Meänkieli is a close relative of the Finnish language, and is spoken by the Tornedale Finns, the majority of whom live in the north of Sweden. Around 70,000 people in Sweden speak or understand Meänkieli, not all of them fluently.

Sami languages Approximately 80,000-100,000 Sami live in Sápmi, which stretches across northern Norway, Sweden, Finland and Russia. Of those, 20,000-40,000 live in Sweden, and an estimated 40-45 percent speak one of the variants of the Sami language. The languages can be traced back to around 0 AD.

Yiddish Thousands of Jews arrived in Sweden in the 18th century, and now there are around 15,000–20,000 Jews living in Sweden, mainly in the larger cities. Their minority language is Yiddish.

Romani There are 50,000–100,000 Roma living across Sweden. The different variations of Romani constitute the final minority language of Sweden. The language has been spoken in Sweden since the 16th century, although there was a centuries-long lapse when the Roma community was outlawed from Sweden, when many fled to Finland.

Tjena 'Hey' INTERJECTION

ɕeːna

In Sweden you can never go wrong with a simple *hej* as a greeting. But this is another way of saying 'hello'.

Whether you're talking to your friend, a child, an adult, your boss or a complete stranger — *hej* always works, and is the safest bet if you are not sure what level of formality to aim for.

But if you're confident enough to branch out into the world of slang, you may want to consider going for a *tjena*. *Tjena* is more familiar than *hej* and is not appropriate for greeting a prospective employer in a job application, but as Swedish is not a particularly formal language, it works in nearly all other contexts.

Tjena is short for *tjenare* (somtimes spelled *tjänare*). This means 'servant', and the greeting can be traced back to around 1775 in its longer version *mjuka tjänare* ('humble servant').

Nowadays, few Swedes reflect on this archaic meaning of what is considered an informal greeting phrase rather than a subservient way of showing civility and deference to a very important person.

Other, even more informal, variants of *tjena* include *tjenixen*, *tjenamors*, *tjabba* or *tja*.

Tjena kexet, står du här och smular?
Hey there biscuit, are you standing here crumbling?*

Tjena Olle, det var inte i går!
Hi there Olle, long time no see!

* A Swedish pick-up line based on the fact that the word *kex* can refer both to a biscuit and to an attractive person.

Tjomme **'Guy' (Gothenburg dialect)** NOUN

ɕʊmːɛ

If you're living in Gothenburg, or planning to visit the west coast city at some point, it's a good idea to learn some of the local dialect.

Gothenburg, known as Sweden's second, arguably 'friendlier' port city (and often dubbed 'Little London') has a distinct dialect: *göteborgska*.

One word that you may find elsewhere in Sweden, but that has its roots in the west coast city, is the informal *tjomme*, which means 'guy' or 'mate'. Synonyms in Swedish are *karl*, *man*, *snubbe*, *kille*, or *kompis*.

The word derived from the English 'chummy', which is student slang for 'chamber-fellow' or roommate.

A poll of 1,000 Swedes conducted by the Swedish Institute for Opinion Surveys (*Svenska institutet för opinionsundersökningar, SIFO*) found that Swedes find the dialect spoken in Gothenburg to be the sexiest of all Swedish dialects. All the more reason to become acquainted with the regional tongue.

Alla undrar vad det är för en tjomme.
Everybody wonders what kind of guy this is.

Det stod en tjomme utanför lägenheten.
A guy was standing outside the apartment.

Tomte 'Scandinavian gnome' or 'Father Christmas/ Santa Claus' NOUN

tɔmːtɛ

Tomte is the name for a gnome-like creature in Nordic folklore, and in Sweden, it's the *jultomte* ('Christmas *tomte*') who is the traditional bringer of gifts on Christmas Eve (not Christmas Day).

The word *tomte* comes from the term *en tomt* (a plot of land). In Nordic folklore, each *tomt* had a small gnome-like creature to look after the area and use its special powers to ensure good luck for those who lived there, and this creature was called a *tomte*.

According to some traditions, the *tomte* was the spirit of the very first owner of the plot of farmland, and they were generally described as resembling an elderly human man, usually with a long white beard, but smaller than a person.

You need to watch out for the *tomte* though, as they are believed to have a short fuse and can be vindictive, so farmers would often leave out porridge for the creature around Christmas, in order to pacify them.

Tomte is used in several different ways in Swedish. You might jokingly refer to someone with a long beard, or who performs many different practical tasks, as a *tomte*, and the phrase *ha tomtar på loftet* ('to have *tomtar* in the attic') means to be slightly crazy. Sparklers are referred to as *tomtebloss* ('gnome smoke').

Around Christmas time, the traditional figure of the *tomte* has become slightly conflated with the Father Christmas or Santa Claus of other countries to become the *jultomte* ('Christmas *tomte*') who brings presents to well-behaved children. And in homes and shops across the country you'll find small toys and models depicting the festive bearded *tomte*.

Tror du på jultomten?
Do you believe in Santa?

Jultomten är en sammanblandning av Sankt Nikolaus, Santa Claus och hustomten.
The Swedish *jultomte* is a mix of St. Nicholas, Santa Claus and the *tomte*.

Trivas **'To feel comfortable'** VERB

tri:vas

Trivas has no neat one-word English translation, but means something like 'to feel settled', 'to be comfortable' or 'to feel at home'.

If you're a recent arrival in Sweden, expect to be asked *Trivs du i Sverige?* ('Do you feel at home in Sweden/are you enjoying life in Sweden?') by your local friends and colleagues. It can be used to talk about feeling comfortable and happy in any place or environment, such as a city, house, university, or a workplace.

The environment doesn't have to be a concrete one. You can say, for example *Jag trivs i mitt eget sällskap* ('I'm happy in my own company'), *Jag trivs med att jobba i ett nära team* ('I like working in a close team'), or *Jag trivs med att hålla många bollar i luften* ('I like having lots of projects on the go').

You'll also see the noun form, *trivsel*, for example: *Det är viktigt att skapa trivsel på jobbet* ('It's important to create well-being/contentment/a sense of belonging at work' or 'It's important to create a positive work environment').

But *trivas* doesn't have to refer to a person, or even to a conscious sense of comfort and happiness. You can also say things like *Blåbär trivs bäst i granskog* ('Bilberries grow best in spruce forest'), or *Virus trivs i kallare slemhinnor* ('Viruses thrive in cool mucous membranes'). In these cases, it can be helpful to think of *trivas* as meaning 'to thrive' — the two words are related.

In fact, both *trivas* and English 'thrive' are descendants of the Old Norse term *þrifa*, which meant something like 'to clasp/ to grasp'. This became *þrifask* in a reflexive form, first meaning 'to grasp closely to oneself' and later coming to mean 'to thrive'. Danish and Norwegian both use the verb *trives* in a very similar way to Swedish *trivas* too.

Jag vill att du ska trivas i vår vackra stad.
I want you to feel at home in our beautiful town.

Jag har alltid trivts i hans sällskap.
I have always felt comfortable with him.

Trotsåldern 'The age of defiance' NOUN

trɔt:sɔl:dɛɳ

Trotsåldern is the age of toddler tantrums, what in English-speaking countries is known as 'the terrible twos', but which often extends to three and four-year-olds too.

It is a compound word combining *trots*, meaning 'defiance' (note: *trots* is also a preposition meaning 'despite') and *åldern* meaning 'the age of', so it literally means 'the age of defiance'.

It is used most often in Sweden as a one-word excuse from embarrassed parents as their child lies shrieking on a supermarket floor, red-faced, hammering the ground, and refusing to be moved.

For example: [sighs]... *det är ju trotsåldern*. This could be translated as '... it's just the terrible twos, you know'.

Trotsåldern is also the subject of innumerable articles in newspapers, magazines and parenting blogs with titles like: *Hur man hanterar barn i trotsåldern* ('How to handle children in the terrible twos'), *Myten om trotsåldern* ('The myth of the terrible twos'), and *Så överlever ni trotsåldern* ('How you survive the terrible twos').

You will sometimes hear the word *trotsig* ('defiant') applied to toddlers in *trotsåldern*, although it can equally describe a rebellious teenager, a stubborn animal, or a stubborn adult.

And you can also talk about *trotsåldrar* ('ages of defiance'), *tvåårstrots* ('two-year-old defiance'), *treårstrots* ('three-year-old defiance'), and even *tonårstrots* ('teenage defiance').

Med ett barn i trotsåldern ställs stora krav på dig.
When you have a child in the terrible twos, it demands a lot of you.

Den klassiska trotsåldern börjar omkring två och ett halvt år.
The classic terrible twos starts at around two and a half years old.

Tråkig **'Boring'; 'sad'** ADJECTIVE

tro:kɪ

Tråkig usually appears in dictionaries as the Swedish equivalent of 'boring' or 'dull', but it's not always easy to translate directly.

Tråkig is more versatile than English 'boring', and is often used generally to describe something bad, sad, unpleasant, or annoying.

For example, if your bike is stolen or you injure yourself, a Swede might say *oj, vad tråkigt.* They're not telling you that your bad luck is boring them; it's a sympathetic expression, which in English we might translate as 'Oh no, how annoying/sad' or 'oh, what a pain'.

This is especially true in the expression *tråkigt nog*, which means 'sadly', as in: *Tråkigt nog finns det många exempel på ojämlikhet i världen* ('Sadly, there are many examples of inequality in the world').

But in other situations, *tråkig* can be ambiguous. For example, if you share an anecdote with Swedish friends and they reply *Det var en tråkig historia* ('That was a sad/boring story'), you'll need to rely on clues such as their tone and the general context to work out what they mean.

If you want to be clear that you mean 'boring/tedious', you can use the word *långtråkig*, a more emphatic form of *tråkig*.

Tråkig comes from an old Swedish verb, *tråka*, which originally meant 'to push together/to clamp' and is related to the words *trycka* ('to push') and *tryck* ('pressure') in today's Swedish.

Over time, the meaning of this word developed from referring to physical pushing to metaphorical pushing, in the sense of going over and over the same point. From there, it soon came to mean 'to walk/move slowly' and was also used to mean 'to work slowly'.

Today, *tråka* survives in the phrasal verb *tråka ut*, meaning 'to bore', for example: *Jag ska inte tråka ut dig med alla detaljer* ('I won't bore you with all the details').

Vi läser en dödstråkig bok i skolan.
We're reading a deathly boring book at school.

Det var tråkigt att höra att din hund är försvunnen.
It was sad (note: not boring!) to hear that your dog's gone missing.

Tupplur **'Nap'** NOUN

tɵpːlʉːr

A *tupplur* is a short period of sleep, usually during daytime. To use it in a sentence you'd use the phrase *ta en tupplur* ('to take/have a nap'). It's a compound noun, made up of two different words: *tupp* + *lur*.

Lur on its own can be used to mean 'nap' or 'doze', although it also has several other meanings, including 'bell' or 'horn'.

The strange part of *tupplur* is *tupp*, which means 'cock' — 'a male chicken'.

According to the word experts at the Swedish Language Council, the term comes from the fact that chickens tend to sleep in short periods, often while standing. An earlier Swedish word for nap, in fact, was *hönssömn*, literally meaning 'chicken sleep', and similar nouns are found in Norwegian (*høneblund*), Danish (*hønsesøvn*) and Icelandic (*hænublundur*).

Tupplur is believed to date back to at least the early 1800s, and is a common word in Swedish. It's not that surprising if you consider that the Nordic nations were agricultural economies for much longer than many other European countries.

In English, meanwhile, the usual animal-inspired term for a short sleep is 'cat nap', based on the fact that cats often doze for just a few minutes at a time, although in total they sleep far more than chickens.

If you're looking for more poultry-themed idioms, the Swedish language has a plentiful supply: early-risers might say they're *uppe med tuppen* ('up with the cockerel'), and one way of describing someone who is very proud of their achievements is to say they're *stolt som en tupp* ('proud as a rooster').

In Swedish, you'll also hear the English loan word *powernap* (all one word) used to refer to especially short snoozes, and the direct translation *kraftlur* is also sometimes used in spoken or online Swedish.

Jag är jättetrött, jag måste ta en tupplur och sen en kopp kaffe.
I'm really tired, I need to take a nap and then have a cup of coffee.

Är det okej att ta en tupplur på jobbet?
Is it OK to take a nap at work?

Uppesittarkväll 'The sitting-up evening' NOUN

ɵpːɛsɪtakfɛlː

Did you know that the Swedes have a special name for the night before the night before Christmas?

In fact, make that three names. But we'll start with *uppesittarkväll*.

Uppesittarkväll can be translated as 'sitting-up evening' which captures the sense of anticipation ahead of the big event. This is because Swedes have their main Christmas celebration on December 24th, Christmas Eve in English or *julafton*. So the day before, the 23rd, youngsters might be unable to sleep, while adults are usually busy with the preparations of food and decorations.

Uppesittarkväll is also the name given to a range of special TV and radio programmes on the 23rd, which are shown on several channels and serve as background entertainment to the festive preparations.

Watching these is a good initiation to Swedish Christmas traditions: guests discuss tips for a perfect celebration, and often write rhyming verses for gift tags (an old Swedish custom — the rhyme should give a clue as to the present inside) alongside musical performances and competitions.

As for the other two names for December 23rd, in the southern region of Skåne, it is known as *lillejulafton* ('little Christmas Eve').

Elsewhere and especially among the older generations, you'll hear the 23rd called *dan före dopparedan*, which means 'the day before dipping day'.

Dopparedan or 'dunking day' is an alternative name for Christmas Eve thanks to an old custom of eating *dopp i grytan* ('dunk in stew' referring to flatbread or rye bread dunked in a meaty broth) as part of the festive evening meal. But neither of these truly captures the magic and excitement in the same way as *uppesittarkväll.*

Ska vi titta på uppesittarkväll på tv?
Shall we watch the December 23rd show on TV?

Hon har bjudit in sina vänner på uppesittarkväll.
She has invited her friends round on the evening of December 23rd.

Utedass 'Outdoor toilet' NOUN

ʉ:tɛdas:

Utedass comes from *ute* ('outside') and *dass* (an informal term for 'toilet') and it is a common feature of the Swedish summer, even today. You might also hear it called a *torrdass*, a 'dry toilet', or someone might direct you to the *lilla huset* ('the little building').

An *utedass* looks like a small shed, and you'll find them in Swedish nature reserves and along hiking trails to allow walkers to answer the call of nature.

But that's not all: many Swedes own or have access to a summer cabin, and it's not unusual for the *utedass* to be the only available toilet, since many of the more basic *stugor* don't have plumbing.

What might surprise you is that an *utedass* is often seen as a bonus rather than a downside; some families are really proud of them and will make them feel cosy with decor and brightly coloured paint.

Sweden may be a technologically advanced country, but as a nation that's largely covered in forest, and which underwent industrialisation relatively late, many people who live here are fond of going back to basics and connecting with nature.

This is summed up in the Scandinavian term *friluftsliv* ('open air life') and is clear from the popularity of isolated summer houses and hiking.

But if it's not your thing, rest assured that plenty of Swedish *stugor* these days come equipped with modern luxuries including flushing toilets.

På tomten finns en liten stuga med utedass.
On the plot of land there is a small cabin and an outdoor toilet.

Att använda utedass är en del av friluftslivet.
Using an outdoor toilet is part of outdoor life.

Crossword

Test yourself to see how many words you remember from the book.

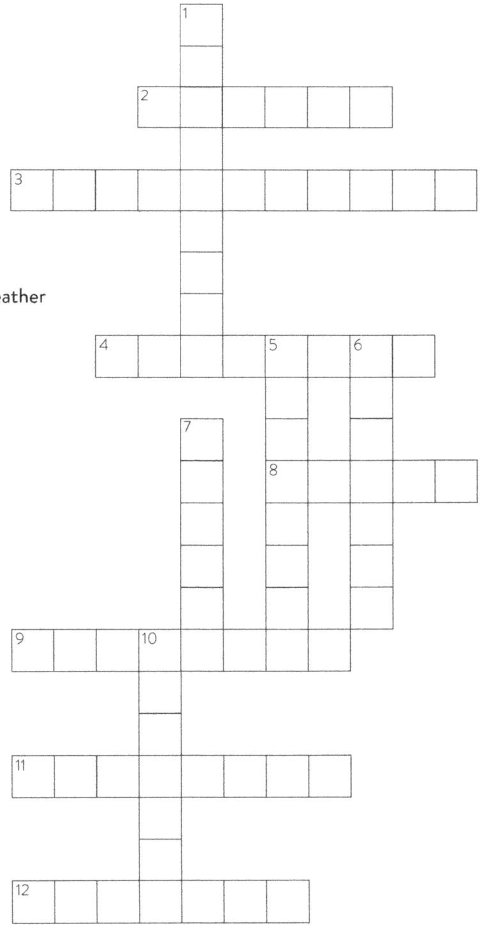

Across
2. idiot
3. traditional Swedish food
4. damp and unpleasant autumnal weather
8. gladly
9. someone who doesn't like swimming
11. Stockholmer
12. nap

Down
1. candy cane
5. potato pancake
6. Sweden
7. bad weather
10. release of the cows

Answer key on lysforlag.com/vvv

Uteservering 'Outdoor cafe or restaurant terrace'

NOUN

u:tɛsɛrveːrɪŋ

At a certain point in the early spring, you'll see bars, cafes and restaurants setting up chairs and tables out on the pavement: this is the *uteservering*.

You can break the word down into *ute* ('outdoors') and *servering* (which means both 'restaurant' and 'the act of serving'). It covers everything from rooftop bars to cafe courtyards to kiosks in parks with tables and chairs, and they usually open from around early April to September: local regulations usually define when the *uteservering* season can take place. Even on chilly days probably best spent inside, you'll see locals stubbornly wrapped in blankets (provided by the restaurant) and eating their meal under an outdoor heater rather than waste a moment of daylight.

These days, sipping a cocktail or cold beer at one of these spots is an integral part of Swedish summertime, which fits into the Scandinavian mentality of making the most of those long summer days and nights.

But it wasn't always the case.

The very first *uteservering* in Sweden is said to have been opened in Gothenburg in the mid-19th century. But over the following century, strict laws around alcohol meant a lot of restrictions on restaurants with alcohol permits. Far fewer restaurants were allowed to serve beer, wine and spirits, and even in those, alcohol had to be drunk indoors.

It wasn't until the 1980s that the trend started up again, perhaps influenced by increasing travel overseas and Swedes experiencing cafe terrace culture in places like France and Italy.

In the early 1990s both Gothenburg and Malmö introduced permits at a municipal level for *uteserveringar*. When smoking was banned inside restaurants about ten years later, new permits were introduced allowing year-round outdoor areas, and now they are a major fixture of cities in summer.

Det är så mysigt att ta en öl på en uteservering när solen skiner.
It's so nice to have a beer on an outdoor terrace in the sunshine.

De flesta uteserveringar öppnar 1 april.
Most outdoor terraces open on April 1st.

Vabruari **'The month when parents most often have to take time off work to look after sick children'** NOUN

vabrʉɑːrɪ

Vabruari is a portmanteau, a word that combines two others in both sound and meaning. It is made up of *februari* (February), and *VAB*, an acronym which stands for *vård av barn* ('care of [sick] child').

Vab is a benefit paid out to working parents when they need to stay at home to look after a sick child, or accompany them to a doctor or hospital. It's a major part of what makes Sweden a family-friendly place to work, with parents entitled to up to 120 days each year per child (on average, they take around seven per child).

It can be written either as *vab* or *VAB*, and you'll see this great time of the year written as *vabruari* or *VABruari*, but the most common form is all lower case letters (Swedish doesn't capitalise the names of months or weekdays).

In Swedish, you'll hear it used as a verb, *vabba* (*Mattias vabbar idag* — 'Mattias is taking time off to care for his sick child today') and it's so common that you'll hear it used by English speakers in Sweden too ('Mattias is vabbing today'). Not to be confused with *vobba*, which is a portmanteau of *vabba* + *jobba*, meaning to work while looking after a sick child.

But back to *vabruari*. With the year's shortest month bringing unpredictable temperature changes and the peak of the flu and *vinterkräksjuka* ('winter vomiting disease', a form of norovirus), February has typically been the month when parents need the most time off to care for sick children.

It has become a very common word, even if it's only been used over the past decade or two, and will be understood by anyone in Sweden; you'll even see it in writing at doctor's offices or from unions. Some brands use it to advertise vitamins, puzzles or other products that might make the month easier to survive.

Vabruari är här igen – lycka till!
'Vabruary' is here again, good luck!

Februari kallas vabruari av småbarnsföräldrar eftersom barn ofta är sjuka då.
February is called Vabruary by parents of small children because children are often sick around this time of the year.

Varsågod **'You're welcome'** INTERJECTION

va:ʂɔguː

Varsågod is usually translated as 'you're welcome' but can also mean 'please' and/or 'here you go'.

There are three main contexts in which you might hear or use this word.

Firstly, if someone says *tack* ('thank you') to you, you can respond *varsågod* ('you're welcome'). Alternative options in this context might be *ingen orsak* ('no trouble') or *det var så lite så* ('it was nothing'), but *varsågod* is the most common.

It can be used in a passive aggressive way if you don't receive a *tack* when you might expect it. For example if you hold the door open and someone passes through it without a nod or word of thanks, you could mutter *varsågod* under your breath.

The second context for using *varsågod* is when giving something to someone; a waiter might say it as they hand you your dish, or your boss as they pass round out agendas at the start of a meeting. Here, it means something like 'here you go'.

And finally, it can be used as a slightly formal way of saying 'please'.

Swedish doesn't really have a direct translation for 'please': when ordering food, for example, the customer tends to simply say *tack* ('thank you'). But if you want to stress politeness and formality, you can start a sentence with something like *varsågod och…*, which literally means something like 'please be so kind as to…' For example: *Varsågod och sitt* ('please sit down').

You may have already guessed that it can be broken down into three parts: *var så god*, which literally means 'be so good/kind'. French speakers might notice a similarity to the French term for 'please', *s'il vous plaît* (literally: 'if it pleases you').

When addressing groups of more than one person, you use the plural form, *varsågoda*. So if you're in a restaurant, a waiter might show you to your table with the word *varsågod* (if you're on your own) or *varsågoda* (for groups), meaning something like 'please sit down'.

If you use instant messaging or text with Swedes, you can abbreviate the word to *vsg*.

Varsågod och fortsätt.
Please continue.

Om du vill lägga till någonting, varsågod.
If you want to add anything, please go ahead.

***Vovve* 'Doggy'** NOUN

VƱV ː Ɛ

If you're raising bilingual children in Sweden, this may very well be one of the first words they learn as they start to get a sense of the world around them.

While a Swedish dog is usually known as a *hund*, the word *vovve* — or *vovvar* in plural — is commonly used as a more diminutive word in speech directed at children (or by owners talking to their dogs).

Vovve, which the Swedish Academy dates back to 1867, is a form of onomatopoeia — words that imitate the sounds they describe — and comes from the word *vov-vov,* which is the sound a dog makes in Swedish.

You can compare this to for example 'woof' in English or *bau* in Italian.

But why do animals sound different in different languages? As you can probably guess, it is not that the animals are multilingual, but we perceive the sounds in different ways depending on our own language.

There is one theory attributed to German philosopher Johann Gottfried Herder (although this is contested) which suggests that animal sounds contributed to the birth of human language — when our ancestors started imitating the sounds they heard in their natural environment.

Other Swedish animal noises include *kuckeliku*, *nöff* and *gnägg*.

Vovve is also used in the phrase *villa, Volvo, vovve* ('detached house, Volvo, dog'), used by Swedes to sum up the three things that show you've made it as an adult.

Titta, vilken söt liten vovve.
Look, what a cute little dog.

Har du kommit ihåg att mata vovvarna?
Have you remembered to feed the dogs?

Animal sounds

Do Swedish animals speak Swedish? At least according to Swedes, who describe animal sounds slightly differently from English speakers. Are you able to match the sound with the animal?

1. dog	a) ***mjau***
2. cat	b) ***brum***
3. horse	c) ***vov-vov***
4. pig	d) ***pip***
5. frog	e) ***gnägg***
6. mouse	f) ***kvack***
7. bear	g) ***nöff nöff***

1c, 2a, 3e, 4g, 5f, 6d, 7b

Vårstädning 'Communal spring cleaning day' NOUN

vo:ʂtɛ:dnɪŋ

Vårstädning has a simple English translation, but also refers to a very Swedish concept.

Vårstädning (*vår* + *städning*) means 'spring clean' and refers to a big tidy-up at the start of the warmer season. You can do this on your own at home, but in Sweden many housing associations and apartment blocks also organise a *vårstädning* day as a group activity, involving weeding, planting flowers and so on.

There is a lot of housing association politics involved.

It's a chance to get to know the neighbours with coffee and snacks provided for helpers.

And if you choose not to attend, expect to be judged by the neighbours — and be prepared with your excuse if you happen to pass them on your way out of the building.

Sweden is big on collective responsibility and everyone playing their part or at very least appearing to, so these days are when you're expected to show your face.

There's also an autumn counterpart, *höststädning*, when the outdoor furniture gets taken in and the garden cleared up ready for winter.

Sweden is generally considered a tough place to make friends, and to get to know neighbours. It's not that common, for example, to knock on neighbours' doors to introduce yourself as a new arrival, especially in big cities where apartment blocks have a relatively higher turnover of residents.

But participating in these organised chores, as well as getting involved with the association's board itself, is a way to show you're a good neighbour, willing to do your part.

You can also use *vårstäda* as a verb, for example *vårstäda trädgården* ('to give the garden a spring clean').

Fy vad jobbigt, snart är det dags för vårstädning!
Ugh what a pain, it's nearly spring cleaning day!

Kommer du på vårstädningen?
Are you coming to the housing association's cleaning day?

Å '(Medium-sized) river' NOUN/INTERJECTION

O ː

Let's look at one of the Swedish language's single-letter words. *Å* is the 27th letter of the Swedish alphabet, and a surprisingly versatile word.

So what does it mean? A few different things.

En å is the word for a medium-sized river, stream or brook (a smaller stream is called *bäck* and a larger river *älv* or *flod*). The plural of *å* is *åar*.

Å is common in place names, usually meaning the location is near a river. There are a total of 12 locations in Sweden called Å, and several others that use *-å* as a suffix, such as Skogså (literally 'forest brook') and Luleå, Piteå and Skellefteå in northern Sweden.

Å can also be an interjection, similar to 'oh!', and usually expresses joy or surprise, but can sound slightly affected or old-fashioned. For example: *Å, vad jag är glad!* ('Oh, how happy I am!').

In older Swedish, *å* was a preposition equivalent to 'on' in English. Today it has been mostly replaced by *på*, but you will still see *å* in some set phrases such as *å ena sidan… å andra sidan* ('on the one hand… on the other hand') or *å någons vägnar* ('on someone's behalf'). In the latter phrase, you can also use *på*.

Jag ser en å där borta.
I can see a stream over there.

Hon var å andra sidan jätteduktig.
On the other hand, she was very competent.

Word search puzzle

We have included 30 Swedish words from this book in the word search puzzle. Words are placed horizontally, vertically and diagonally, and can be read forwards and backwards. How many can you find?

K	H	M	H	U	S	Z	S	V	H	C	O	S	L	E
K	E	K	S	U	R	T	S	Ö	H	D	S	I	I	T
B	J	M	L	D	U	L	D	A	X	U	A	Ö	L	M
Y	S	O	L	G	O	G	S	H	P	C	N	M	L	O
S	C	G	A	P	I	L	Q	A	K	R	R	O	Ö	T
I	G	O	P	K	U	Z	Y	J	I	G	Ä	S	R	D
P	N	I	Å	J	L	R	L	T	R	E	G	T	D	V
F	S	R	G	L	Ö	G	G	G	E	E	F	B	A	Q
R	T	G	Ö	A	J	N	V	H	R	I	D	J	G	T
J	L	H	P	H	X	J	E	O	G	Ö	M	Ä	H	I
A	N	E	J	T	O	N	F	R	V	I	T	F	V	S
K	A	N	E	L	B	U	L	L	E	V	F	Y	N	O
P	G	H	J	M	S	E	M	E	S	T	E	R	U	R
T	R	O	T	S	Å	L	D	E	R	N	J	W	F	P
S	S	A	D	E	T	U	V	A	B	R	U	A	R	I

Answer key on lysforlag.com/vvv

Ålahue 'Idiot' (Skåne dialect) NOUN

o:lahʉ:ɛ

The residents of Skåne don't take fools gladly, and that's reflected in the local language. The inhabitants of Sweden's southernmost county have as many ways of calling someone stupid as the indigenous peoples of the Arctic have for snow (almost).

Chief among these is *ålahue*.

A compound noun composed of the word *ål*, meaning 'eel', and *hue*, the Scanian (*skånska*) dialect form of the Swedish *huvud* or 'head', *ålahue* means, literally, 'eel head'.

It requires the correct pronunciation to achieve full effect, beginning with a vowel like the beginning of 'elephant' in English and dipping almost immediately into the start of 'oops' before hitting the 'l' sound.

Mathias Strandberg, an expert in Scanian dialect at Sweden's Institute for Language and Folklore, told *The Local* the word probably had its roots in the local eel fisheries.

Strandberg believes the word is new in its current form, as Scanian only developed *hue* as a common word for head relatively recently.

The phrase can be used as a pejorative whenever someone is performing a task poorly or displays ignorance.

Så kan du ju inte göra, ditt ålahue!
You can't do it that way, you idiot!

Skåne tillhörde Danmark på den tiden, ditt ålahue!
Scania belonged to Denmark in those days, you fool!

Åsiktskorridor 'Corridor of opinions' NOUN

o:sɪktskɔrɪdo:r

The word *åsiktskorridor* is crucial if you want to get along with Swedes, whether in a professional or personal context.

It means 'opinion corridor' or 'corridor of opinions', from *en åsikt* ('view/opinion') and *korridor* ('corridor').

It's used to talk about the range of different opinions that are socially acceptable to share or to hold on a subject.

Åsiktskorridor is a recently coined term, its first known use being in 2009. It was later defined by political science professor Henrik Oscarsson, who was describing the subjects that it's acceptable to put up for debate.

If a topic is outside the *åsiktskorridor*, it is viewed as too extreme or divisive to debate, and therefore rarely brought up in conversation, especially among people who don't know each other well. Playing devil's advocate rarely goes down well in Swedish circles.

On one hand, the *åsiktskorridor* could in theory help to keep extreme views such as racism or homophobia outside the mainstream. It helps to avoid giving airtime to people who are arguing against something that has been proven as fact, such as climate change deniers or conspiracy theorists.

The problem that Oscarsson raised was that many people may still hold opinions outside the 'corridor', so if the *åsiktskorridor* is too narrow, people lose out on the chance for constructive debate and free speech in favour of the Swedish preference for consensus. One risk, he argued, is that if people with views outside the mainstream feel they can't voice them in general society, they will be pushed towards fringe or extreme groups instead.

The phenomenon isn't limited to Sweden, and concepts like 'political correctness' and 'echo chamber' in English show there's an understanding that people tend to surround themselves with people who hold similar views, and only share opinions which they believe are held by the majority in the group, in other cultures too.

Det är inte bra om åsiktskorridoren blir för smal.
It's not good if the opinion corridor gets too narrow.

Är åsiktskorridoren i Sverige myt eller verklighet?
Is the opinion corridor in Sweden a myth or reality?

Ö 'Island' NOUN

ø:

The Swedish language may be known for its lengthy and complex words, but we'll end with one that's just one letter long.

Ö is the 29th and final letter of the Swedish alphabet — unlike in German, for example, it's a distinct letter and not an accented *o*. Swedes are very proud of their 29th letter.

Note that in Swedish, instead of saying 'A to Z' you say *A till Ö*. Of the Scandinavian languages, Swedish and Icelandic are the only ones with the letter *ö*.

It's also a word in its own right, meaning 'island'.

Sweden has a long coastline and many, many lakes, so it's a word you'll hear a lot.

You'll spot it in place names of course, like Värmdö, Djurö, Älgö, Hönö and Björkö (literally meaning 'hot spring island', 'animal island', 'elk island', 'hen island' and 'birch tree island'). These are generally Sweden's smaller islands, while big ones like Gotland have names without the *ö*. An exception is Öland, Sweden's second largest island — here the 'land' emphasises the larger size.

You generally use the preposition *på* with islands: *jag bor* på *Värmdö* instead of *jag bor* i *Värmdö*.

The word for 'peninsula' is *halvö*, 'half island'.

Ö also features in a Swedish dialectal poem, *Dumt fôlk* ('Stupid people' by Gustaf Fröding) in a line made up of single letters. The sentence goes: "*d'ä e å, å i åa ä e ö*". In standard Swedish, that's "*det är en å, och i ån är en ö*" ('there is a stream, and in the stream there is an island'). If that confuses you, don't worry — the whole point of the poem is about a city visitor failing to understand the dialect!

Jag bor på en liten ö i skärgården.
I live on a small island in the archipelago.

Ingen människa är en ö.
No person is an island.

IPA Guide

Swedish pronunciation in more detail

STRESS

The most important thing to focus on when learning basic Swedish pronunciation is stress. Stress is marked with a long syllable, and within that syllable, there is either a long vowel sound or a long consonant sound. In this book, stress is marked with a ː placed directly after the long sound.

There may be one or two stressed syllables in a Swedish word.

choklad	ɧʊkl ɑːd	ː after *a* means a long *a* sound: *choklaaaaad*
tårta	toːʈa	ː after *å* gives a long *å* sound: *tååååårta*
chokladtårta	ɧʊkl ɑːdtoːʈa	in compound words, there are two stressed syllables, in this case a long *a* and a long *å* sound: *choklaaaaadtååååårta*

We cannot stress enough how important stress is, and how much more it matters than individual sounds. Still, we know many learners are keen on mastering their *å*s and *ä*s and *ö*s like a native, which is why we have put together this guide. There is no perfect way of explaining the sounds of one language using the writing system of another, but, arguably, the best option is the IPA (International Phonetic Alphabet), which we have used alongside examples in Swedish and English approximations.

Bear in mind, though, that even though English and Swedish have a handful of sounds in common, these are rarely direct equivalents. The best way to find out what Swedish really sounds like is to listen. You can find the audio files on lysforlag.com/vvv

VOWEL SOUNDS

Swedish is infamous for its many vowel sounds, and it may take some time to recognise all of them. In general, Swedish is mostly produced in the front of your mouth, with more noticeable lip movements than in English, and there are significant differences between stressed and unstressed vowels.

	Example	English approximation
a	*j**a**ha, j**a**j**a**mens**a**n*	somewhere between bl**u**nt and bl**a**nd.

a is always short, sometimes in a stressed syllable, followed by a long consonant sound, and sometimes in an unstressed syllable. There are only two exceptions to this: you find a long a : in the informal greeting *tja* and the swearword *fan*. Spelled *a*.

ɑ :	*jah**a**, kollektivavt**a**l*	c**a**lm and sm**a**rt

ɑ : is always stressed, that is long, and slightly different in quality to a. To get the ɑ : sound right, imagine you're an opera singer, or that your dentist is examining your molars. Open your mouth as much as you can, as a vertically oriented ovoid, and start practising your vocal scales. Spelled *a*.

ø :	*gr**ö**t, sn**ö**mos*	ever h**ea**rd these w**o**rds?

In terms of lip movements, ø : is not that different from ɑ : . Keep your mouth positioned vertically but tighten your lips for a smaller ovoid shape. You should look less like an opera singer and more like a duck. Spelled *ö*.

œ :	*l**ö**rdagsgodis, bj**ö**rntjänst*	undist**u**rbed nature

œ : is what happens to ø : when followed by an *r*. It's a rounder, more open sound. The duck grows a bigger beak, simply speaking. Spelled *ö(r)*.

œ	*h**ö**strusk, surstr**ö**mming*	**lea**rning Swedish may h**u**rt

œ is, roughly, the short, or unstressed, version of œ : . Spelled *ö*.

i: *munsbit, polkagris* freezing winters

Smile. Smile as much as you can and you will master your Swedish i:. Remember i: is always stressed, that is, long, so keep smiling. Spelled *i*.

ɪ *brittsommar, duktig* introvert people

ɪ is the short equivalent of i:, so keep smiling, but not for as long. As you have probably figured out by now, ɪ is always short, sometimes followed by a long consonant sound in a stressed syllable, and sometimes in an unstressed syllable. Spelled *i*.

e: *fredagsmys, kanelbulle* serious business

Keep smiling but open your mouth slightly, like you're posing for a picture and you want to look like you're laughing . e: is always stressed, that is long. Spelled *e*.

ɛ: *oväder, vårstädning* fresh **air**

Keep the big smile of i: and e: but this time open your mouth even more. Imagine someone is about to feed you a huge spoon of your favourite ice cream. Spelled *ä*.

ɛ *björntjänst, deckare* **ex**pensive

ɛ is similar to ɛ: but shorter. This is what you look like when the picture has been taken, right before the smile is gone. Spelled *e* or *ä*.

æ: *gärna, särbo* married or not

Curiously, ɛ: behaves differently when followed by an *r*. æ: is bigger and rounder, to fit more ice cream. æ: is always stressed. An *ä* followed by an *r* gives you this sound.

æ *Sverige, Värmland* avoid the tourist traps

æ is always short version of æ:. Spelled *e* or *ä* followed by an *r*.

uː	*j**o**, kr**o**g*	w**oo**llen jumpers

uː is always stressed, that is long. Round your lips into a small circle pointing straight ahead. Spelled *o*.

ʊ	*tj**o**mme, v**o**vve*	beautiful w**oo**ds

Like uː but shorter. Spelled *o*.

oː	*l**o**v, påt**å**r*	**o**rderliness

oː is similar to uː, but imagine you're pointing your lips more, like you're admiring a cute *vovve* with an 'awww'. Spelled *o* or *å*.

ɔ	*d**o**pp, noll**å**tta*	t**o**p n**o**tch

Like oː but shorter. Spelled *o* or *å*.

ʉː	*badkr**u**ka, dammss**u**gare*	right between m**oo**dy and c**u**te

Now we're getting to the real gymnastics of Swedish vowel sounds. Imagine you're about to blow out a candle. Then move your (imaginary) candle to eye height. The result should give a protruding lower lip and a beautiful ʉː sound. Spelled *u*.

ʉ	*vabr**u**ari, kängur**u***	no need to wear a s**ui**t

Like ʉː but shorter. Spelled *u*.

ɵ	*f**u**nkis, g**u**mma*	avoiding disp**u**te

This is what you look like right after having blown out that candle. Your face should be completely relaxed. Spelled *u*.

yː	*f**y**, fredagsm**y**s*	between c**u**te and del**e**te

Go get yourself a pencil. Or a pen, or a toothbrush. Place it horizontally between your mouth and your nose, and then curve your upper lip upwards until you can let go of your hands and your pencil stays put where it is. Then say 'eeeee'. If this fails, you lack the necessary muscles. If you succeed, it's time for a selfie.

ʏ	*gr**y**m, m**y**ndighet*	even c**u**ter

Like yː but shorter. Practice makes perfect. Spelled *y*.

CONSONANT SOUNDS

As opposed to the vowel sounds, Swedish consonant sounds are fairly similar to the English equivalents. As usual, pay attention to stress. In stressed syllables with short vowels, the consonants are made long. Otherwise, they are short.

	Example	English approximation
b	***b**ostadsrättsförening* Spelled *b*.	**b**lond
d	***d**opp* Spelled *d*.	**d**ads pushing prams
ɖ	*lö**rd**agsgodis* Try to move the position of your *d* sound further back and pronounce a *d* with your tongue almost touching your palate right behind your front teeth. This is called a retroflex, and this is what happens with some consonants following an *r*. Spelled *rd*.	retroflex *d*
f	***f**ettisdagen* Sometimes, when a *v* is preceded by a voiceless consonant, such as *k*, *s* or *t*, it will sound more like an *f*. Spelled *f* (and sometimes *v*).	**f**lat-pack **f**urniture
g	***g**ubbe* Spelled *g*.	**g**reen is king
h	***h**elg* Spelled *h*.	**h**erring
j	***j**ul* Watch out here so that your Swedish *j*s are soft enough, like the English 'y'. Spelled *j*, *g* followed by *e*, *i*, *y*, *ä or ö* , and *g* preceded by *l* or *r*.	**y**ellow and blue
k	***k**osläpp* To make your Swedish k sound perfect, add a puff of air right after, which in linguist lingo is called 'aspiration'. Spelled *ck* or *k*, rarely *c*. In certain instances, when a *g* is followed by a voiceless consonant, it sounds like *k*.	**c**offee and **c**onsensus

l *lov* liquorice
The Swedish l is produced with the tip of your tongue really close to your teeth, not as far back as the English equivalent. Spelled *l*.

ɭ *ärlig* retroflex *l*
Try to move the position of your *l* sound further back and say *l* with the tip of your tongue touching your palate. Expect a thick, American-sounding *l*. Spelled *rl*.

m ***m**unsbit* **m**eatballs
Spelled *m*.

n ***n**ajs* **N**ordic **N**oir
Spelled *n*.

ɳ *gä**rn**a* retroflex *n*
Another retroflex. Use the same technique as for a normal *n*, and move it backwards so that your tongue touches your palate right behind your front teeth. Spelled *rn*.

ŋ *lu**gn*** dri**n**king so**ng**s
Not difficult for English speakers, but beware there is no *g* sound in the combination ŋn (*gn*). Spelled *ng*, *g* followed by *n*, or *n* followed by *k*.

p ***p**olkagris* **p**rogressive **p**olitics
The Swedish p is very similar to the English equivalent but usually followed by a short aspiration. Spelled *p* or sometimes b (together with a voiceless consonant, such as *t*).

r *t**r**åkig*
ɾ ***r**ötmånad* reindeer and moose
Never worry about your Swedish *r*s. There are many versions, dependent on regions and individuals, so you can simply choose which r sound you are the most comfortable with. Spelled *r*.

s ***s**eme**s**ter* **s**now
In English, an *s* between two vowels is voiced, whereas in Swedish, it is always voiceless. Similarly, *z* is always pronounced like a voiceless *s*. Spelled *c*, *s* or *z*.

ʂ *su**rs**trömming* retroflex *s*

Another opportunity to practise your retroflex skills. A standard s sound is produced with the tip of your tongue touching your teeth. Now, move it half an inch backwards so that it touches the your palate right behind your front teeth, and apply your usual technique for saying ‘s’, and you will produce a thicker sound, like flushing water. Spelled *rs*.

ɧ ***sj**ö* [translated to Scottish as] lo**ch**

This is all Swedish learners’ biggest fear. One way of learning to pronounce ɧ is to whisper a long o and then increase air pressure. In some dialects ɧ is pronounced as ʃ and some learners substitute ɕ for ɧ, for which no one blames them. Don’t panic about this sound; you will still make yourself understood if you don’t master it completely. It can be tricky to spot in writing though, as it can be spelled in a variety of ways: *sj*, *stj*, *j*, *g*, *ch*, as well as *sk* followed by *e*, *i*, *y*, *ä or ö*.

t ***t**om**t**e* **t**icks and mosqui**t**oes

The Swedish t is very similar to the English equivalent but usually followed by a short aspiration. Spelled *t*.

ʈ *princesstå**rt**a* retroflex *t*

Your last chance to explore the beauty of retroflex sounds. Again, locate your technique for producing a standard t and move it backwards so that the tip of your tongue is touching your palate right behind your front teeth. Spelled *rt*.

ɕ ***tj**ena* Swedi**sh** **Ch**ef

ɕ is a source of confusion for many Swedish language learners. But don’t despair, ɕ is not that different from the English ‘sh’ sound, but produced with the tip of your tongue a bit closer to your teeth. It is usually spelled *tj*, *kj* or *k* followed by *e*, *i*, *y*, *ä or ö*.

v	***v**illa, **v**olvo, **v**o**vv**e* Spelled *v* or *w*.	**v**ery good book

Acknowledgements

The words in *Villa Volvo Vovve: The Local's Word Guide to Swedish Life* were originally written for www.thelocal.se by the journalists below, and adapted by the editors and publisher for this book. Thank you to everyone who contributed. Thank you also to Chiara Milford and Isabella Anderson who helped proofread the initial drafts and contributed ideas, our colleagues at The Local and LYS förlag, and most of all The Local's readers whose feedback always helps us improve.

Catherine Edwards: *A, AW, Badkruka, Björntjänst, Bostadsrättsförening, Brittsommar, Dagis, Dammsugare, Deckare, Dopp, Dricks, Duktig, Eller hur, Fettisdagen, Fredagsmys, Funkis, Fy, Gärna, Gift, Glögg, Grym, Gröt, Halka, Hej, Helg, Hemsk, Hen, Husmanskost, Hörni, Höst, Jaha, Jajamänsan, Jul, Julklapp, Julgransplundring, Kille, Kollektivavtal, Kosläpp, Krog, Lillördag, Loppis, Lov, Lugn, Lördagsgodis, Matte & husse, Medelsvensson, Mellandagar, Munsbit, Myndighet, Mörk, Najs, Nja, Ockerhyra, Oj, Oväder, Polkagris, Prosit, Puss, Påskris, Påtår, Raggmunk, Rolig, Rötmånad, Semester, Skog, Skål, Smörgås, Snapsvisa, Snömos, Stuga, Surströmming, Sverige, Sambo & Särbo, Tomte, Trivas, Tråkig, Tupplur, Uppesittarkväll, Utedass, Uteservering, Vabruari, Varsågod, Vårstädning, Å, Åsiktskorridor, Ö*

Emma Löfgren: *Jo, Leg, Nämen, Tjej, Tjena, Vovve*

Richard Orange: *Nollåtta, Spissflabbad, Trotsåldern, Ålahue*

Nele Schröder: *Gubbe & gumma, Kanelbulle*

Louise Nordström: *Höstrusk, Orka*

Anne Grietje Franssen: *Tjomme*

All extra content developed by **LYS förlag**.

Online Resources

Say it in Swedish Casual and fun Swedish lessons, some of it completely free. On most social media channels (@sayitinswedish) and on sayitinswedish.com

Swedishmadeeasy High-quality one-to-one Swedish language tuition, verb bootcamps and pronunciation training, all online with Dr. Anneli B. Haake. swedishmadeeasy.com

InLingo Swedish courses in Malmö and online. inlingo.se

SweTeach Swedish courses online and in Gothenburg, and other online resources with a personal touch. Focus on interaction and conversational skills. sweteach.se

Newbie Guide to Sweden Comprehensive resource about moving to and living in Sweden. Free content and paid online courses. thenewbieguide.se

Two Guys Three Crowns Podcast about what it's really like to live in Stockholm, Sweden, produced by two American expats. 2guys3crowns.se

Life in the Land of the Ice and Snow Podcast on Swedish life including interviews with interesting members from the international community in Sweden. iceandsnow.se

Scandinavia Box/Sverigepaketet Your gateway to Scandinavian products in the United States. scandinaviabox.com

Searching Scandinavia A beginner's genealogy course to help you discover and celebrate your Swedish heritage. theswedishgenealogist.com

The Local Sweden Swedish news in English, as well as features and how-to guides related to living in Sweden. thelocal.se

Printed Resources

Teach Yourself Complete Swedish: Beginner to Intermediate Course by **Anneli B. Haake** A self-study guide in English for anyone who wants to learn Swedish.

Behind Blue Eyes by **CS Duffy** A psychological thriller may not be the expected way to learn about Sweden, but this one gives you great insight into Swedish culture and society, seen from a young English woman's perspective.

Lagom: The Swedish Art of Balanced Living by **Linnéa Dunne** and ***Lagom: The Swedish Secret of Living Well*** by **Lola Akinmade Åkerström** These two books may look similar, and do indeed have an identical title. However, they are both worth reading, given the authors' opposite perspective. Dunne is a Swede living in Ireland, and Åkerström has made the move from Nigeria and the US to Sweden.

Working in Sweden: The A–Z Guide by **Anne Pihl** and **Sofi Tegsveden Deveaux**. This is one of many books on Swedish language and culture by independent publishing house LYS förlag, **lysforlag.com**.